Learning of the Way (*Daoxue*)

Learning of the Way (*Daoxue*):

Self-Cultivation through Neo-Confucian Learning, *Kungfu*, and Martial Arts

JOHN E. YOUNG, PH.D.

ARCHWAY
PUBLISHING

Archway Publishing books may be ordered through booksellers or by contacting:

Archway Publishing
1663 Liberty Drive
Bloomington, IN 47403
www.archwaypublishing.com
1 (888) 242-5904

ISBN: 978-1-4808-3048-6 (sc)
ISBN: 978-1-4808-3049-3 (e)

Library of Congress Control Number: 2016906178

Print information available on the last page.

Archway Publishing rev. date: 6/13/2016

PREFACE

This book was written in an attempt to understand some of the historic and cultural motivations that encouraged individuals to engage in the practice of traditional *wushu* (martial arts) in China. Aside from the self-defense considerations for learning and practicing martial arts, historically there appear to have been other, more fundamental and philosophical considerations for studying martial arts, as well as other arts, in traditional China. These motivations are unknown to most Westerners and were unfamiliar to me when I first began studying *wushu*. In 2009, members of a tai chi discussion group, which was formed in our city, decided to conduct research on several topics related to martial arts, health, and philosophy. At the time, I was aware of the historical importance of Zhu Xi and the topic of Confucian learning.[1] However, I had not specifically researched and written about Confucian learning as it concerns the art and practice of *wushu*. It was at that time that I began investigating what has amounted to a case study of Neo-Confucian concepts and their application to the practice of *wushu*.

When I began my exploration, I found it puzzling that I was unable to locate many previous in-depth case studies, or research, directly relating Neo-Confucian learning principles to *wushu*, or to various other traditional Chinese art forms. I was, however, able to locate some articles and small sections of books on these topics. Nonetheless, I had expected

---

[1] I previously co-authored an article on Confucian learning as it relates to "entrepreneurial learning" (the learning processes entrepreneurs use to grow their businesses). Zhu Xi (Chu Hsi) (1130–1200) is considered the "great synthesizer" of Neo-Confucian philosophy. His ideas dominated not only Chinese thought, but also, significantly influenced the thought of Korea, Japan, Vietnam, and the Chinese diaspora for centuries.

to find a large number of studies linking Neo-Confucian learning principles to specific art forms. Now, after having conducted this study, I am still somewhat puzzled as to why so few contemporary in-depth analyses on this topic are available. This remains one of my primary questions at the conclusion of my inquiry. I will rely on the expertise of traditional Confucian scholars to enlighten me as to the reason for the scarcity of such research. Perhaps such studies and dissertations exist in the Chinese language.

The approach I used in this book is set forth in the table of contents. First, I examine the concept of Confucian learning in general, one of the primary objectives of which is self-cultivation, and explore the major benefits of such self-cultivation. Then I introduce from a historical perspective the era of Neo-Confucianism, which blossomed during the Song (960–1279) and Ming (1368–1644) dynasties. Since Neo-Confucian practice represents the tradition that has had the most significant impact on traditional *wushu*, I investigate these practices (particularly *jing* and *gewu*) in detail. I examine in some depth the approach advocated by the famous Neo-Confucian synthesizer Zhu Xi (1130–1200) because his approach, promoted by the Cheng-Zhu School, became the orthodox perspective in China until the fall of the Qing Dynasty in 1912. The second part of the study applies Confucian and Neo-Confucian concepts introduced in part one, specifically to the art and practice of *wushu*. Part two examines the traditional aspects of *wushu* as they were understood and practiced by many Chinese grandmasters.

Finally, the study attempts to touch upon the potential benefits that the practice of *gongfu* (methodical learning over time, which requires effort) can have on modern, twenty-first-century society. The concept of *guantong* is given special attention since this level of consciousness, recognized historically by Neo-Confucian practitioners, seems particularly relevant in our twenty-first-century world. *Guantong*, a state of consciousness that could be achieved after a long practice of *gongfu*, is described as a "comprehensive understanding" of one's situational context. It represents a state of "integral consciousness." This level of consciousness, in which individuals achieve a sense of impartiality, a sort of aperspective worldview, allowed Neo-Confucians to engage in problem-solving and decision-making in a calm, practical, and effective manner. *Guantong* entails a deep sense of empathy for others. It seems apparent that in our contemporary world, achieving—through sustained effort—a psychological state of empathic impartiality is both urgently needed and more attainable than at any previous time. This research sees the practice of *gongfu*, in this case through traditional *wushu*, as one way or method of raising the consciousness of humankind.

A committed practice of *gongfu*, aimed at revealing and enhancing the humanness or goodness (*ren/jen*) within individual practitioners, could benefit the interconnected web of all beings. *Gongfu* practice, with the intent of augmenting one's own moral development, need not be limited to any geographic region; nor is it dependent on a religious creed. Raising consciousness, and in turn enhancing our humanity and goodness, benefits all living things. A recognition, awareness, and understanding of the basic levels of individual and group consciousness are imperative if humankind is to meet the challenges of an increasingly complex and rapidly changing world. This book suggests that traditional philosophical concepts, drawn from Chinese culture, can help in meeting these challenges. It is my hope that others will continue conducting research along these lines, as the need for consciousness-raising practices is always an imperative.

Finally, I would like to make a few comments regarding some technical aspects of this book. The text is intended to assist in the development of those who are unfamiliar with the academic field of Neo-Confucianism and Confucianism in general. I have attempted to explain and define all terms. Regarding Chinese spellings of names and concepts, I endeavored to present the Pinyin transliteration followed by the Wade-Giles spellings. The Pinyin system of transcribing Mandarin into the Latin alphabet was first adopted by the Chinese government in 1958. The government of Taiwan adopted this system in 2009. The spellings are confusing because most of the early translations of Chinese to English were made using the Wade-Giles system. Since I neither speak nor read Chinese, I imagine that despite my best efforts to ensure the correctness of terms, names, and concepts, some errors may still be present for which I accept full responsibility.

J. E. Y.

ACKNOWLEDGMENTS

Fate indeed takes very interesting turns. I had studied the art of *taijiquan* (also known as *tai chi chuan*) for approximately four years when I met a young student in my class who had recently graduated from Columbia University's Asian Humanities Program. He was so enthusiastic about his recently completed coursework that we met one afternoon to discuss traditional Chinese culture. It was during that single conversation with Gabe Palley, now Dr. Gabriel Palley, M.D., that I first became aware of Neo-Confucianism as an academic field of study. Dr. Palley had taken several classes from Professor Irene Bloom of Columbia, who was also chair of the Department of Asian and Middle Eastern Cultures at Barnard College. Additionally, he had taken seminars from Professor William Theodore de Bary, who had essentially built Columbia's East Asian Studies Program and is credited with creating the specific academic field that is now known as Neo-Confucian Studies. The future Dr. Palley also referred me to the work of the eminent Professor Tu Weiming, professor of philosophy and founding dean of the Institute for Advanced Humanistic Studies at Peking University and senior fellow of the Asia Center at Harvard University. Since I had previously conducted research in the area of entrepreneurial learning, which I feel can serve as a transformational process for successful growth-oriented entrepreneurs, I found the investigation of Confucian learning to be especially interesting.

I would also like to acknowledge the influence of my first teacher of authentic *taijiquan*, Sifu Dug Corpolongo of Albuquerque, New Mexico. My four years of study with Sifu Corpolongo pointed me in the right direction and gave me an appreciation of the dedication that is necessary in order to pursue a path of *gongfu* through *wushu*.

The teacher who has had the most significant influence on the contents of this book has never specifically discussed Neo-Confucian philosophy, as such, with me but has demonstrated in her character and interaction with others the results of *gongfu* and Confucian learning over a lifetime. My primary teacher, with whom I have studied for nearly twenty years, is Master Grace (Xiaogao) Wu-Monnat, founder of the Grace Wu Kung Fu School in Wichita, Kansas. Master Wu has been able to study and learn *wushu* from close family members throughout her life. She is the granddaughter of the famous Chinese Grandmaster Wang Zi-ping (1881–1973). Grandmaster Wang was considered a master of *chaquan*, *huaquan, pao chuan, baijiquan,* and *taijiquan.* He also served as head of the Shaolin Kung Fu division of the Martial Arts Institute in Shanghai. Master Grace Wu-Monnat is a fifth-generation *wushu* practitioner who began studying with her grandfather at the age of three.[2] In the classic Neo-Confucian tradition of *gewu* (the investigation of things), she has published numerous articles and books detailing the *wushu* techniques of her grandfather and *wushu* in general. I am deeply grateful for the instruction and guidance I have received over the years from Master Grace Wu-Monnat. I am also deeply appreciative of the friendship I have developed with Master Wu and her husband, the esteemed and nationally recognized attorney Dan Monnat.[3]

Master Grace Wu-Monnat is the daughter of Professor Wang Ju-rong (1928–2006) and Dr. Wu Chengde, both of whom studied traditional Chinese arts. For example, Dr. Wu, a student of Grandmaster Wang Zi-ping, is a prominent *wushu* master as well as an eminent retired professor of traditional Chinese medicine. Similarly, Grandmaster Wang Ju-rong, Grandmaster Wang Zi-ping's daughter, was the first woman in Chinese history to obtain national certification as a judge in the traditional arts of *wushu* and archery. She practiced *taijiquan, bajiquan, tan tui, chaquan, huaquan,* and *pao chuan,* and was a women's national champion in China. She founded the flying rainbow *taijiquan* fan system. Directly

---

[2] See http://en.wikipedia.org/wiki/Wang_Zi-Ping for more details on the life of Grandmaster Wang Zi-ping.

[3] See http://gracewu.com/biography.html for additional biographical details on Master Grace Wu-Monnat.

pertinent to the contents of this text, Professor Wang Ju-rong was also a consummate practitioner of the tradition of *gewu* (the investigation of things). Over a period of thirty-six years, as a founding professor of the East China Physical Education College in Shanghai, she conducted research on the techniques and theory of *shaolin, taijiquan, tongbeiquan,* and *nanquan.* She was president of the Chinese Martial Arts Research Institute, advisor to the Wu Dang Research Association, and advisor to the Shanghai Qi Gong Research Association.[4] Like my teacher Master Grace Wu-Monnat, Professor Wang Ju-rong's life epitomized the Neo-Confucian concepts and practices described in this text.[5]

I would also like to express my sincere appreciation and gratitude to Mr. Steve Schrankel, my Filipino martial arts instructor for over a decade. His commitment and dedication to the study, practice, and refinement of Asian martial arts has been a personal inspiration to my own martial-arts study, practice, and progress.

Sincere thanks are given to Ms. Jaye Francis for creating the tables and figure presented in the manuscript, as well as George Cross for providing helpful comments and suggestions on earlier versions of the text. I would also like to acknowledge the outstanding editorial assistance I received from Ms. Barbara Scott. Her helpful comments and suggestions significantly improved the quality of the manuscript. Also, I would like to acknowledge the invaluable assistance I received from the staff at Archway Publishing while bringing this book to fruition, particularly Heather Perry as well as Joy T. and Barbara, members of the editing team.

I would like to recognize the impact that my *taiji* (*tai chi*) and *gongfu* (*kungfu*) students have had, not only on this text but also on my personal growth and development. Without their enthusiasm and support, I would not have been able to make the progress that I believe I have made in my own *wushu* practice.

Finally, I want to express my sincere appreciation and gratitude to my wife, Professor Jeanne M. Logsdon, for the encouragement she has

---

[4] See http://en.wikipedia.org/wiki/Wang_Ju-Rong for more details on the life of Grandmaster Wang Ju-Rong.

[5] Professor Wang Ju-rong had three daughters, all of whom are *wushu* masters: Helen (Xiaorong) Wu, Grace (Xiaogao) Wu-Monnat, and Wu Xiaoping.

given to my study of martial arts in general. Without the active support of one's partner, the path of *gongfu* in general must surely be difficult. In addition Jeanne and I have co-authored several publications on consciousness research, some of which are cited in this book. The impact of that exploration is evident throughout this text, and I am indebted to Jeanne for her support and effort in that research stream. Without a doubt, at the time of publication of this manuscript, some errors may still be present and for those I take full responsibility.

CONTENTS

PART 1

Confucian and Neo-Confucian Theory and Concepts

CHAPTER 1

Confucian Self-Cultivation

What Is Confucian Self-Cultivation?

Confucian self-cultivation stems from the basic premise in Confucian philosophy that human beings are innately perfectible through self-effort (Tu 1985). That is to say, humans are born with the capacity to achieve moral excellence. Based upon this fundamental premise, self-cultivation, from the Confucian perspective, is concerned with the ongoing process of striving to achieve moral and spiritual perfection. Furthermore, Confucian self-cultivation is holistic in that it impacts the growth and development of the body, mind, and spirit. Classical Confucian philosophy, which began in ancient times, differs from Neo-Confucian philosophy, which was developed later.

The classical perspective

While numerous scholars have contributed to the body of the Confucian canon, as the tradition has evolved to the present, two scholars in particular influenced the classical perspective. The most important classical scholar was Confucius (551–479 BCE) himself and his sayings as recorded in the *Analects*. The second most influential classical philosopher for this school of thought was Mencius (372–289 BCE). His thoughts are recorded in a text that bears his name, the *Mencius*.

From this classical foundation emerged the underlying concept that if society is in crisis, it is because human beings are inhibited from experiencing their own authentic growth and development. In other words, instead of pursuing individual and societal development, individuals and their respective communities settle for less satisfying and more self-serving goals (Podgorski 1985). Hence, the underlying message is that when authentic human growth and development are impeded, frustration, chaos, and disorder enter society (ibid.).

The Goal of Self-Cultivation

The goal of self-cultivation was to become more human by aiming toward human perfectibility. Mencius' assertion was that the innate goodness of human nature represents the motivating basis for self-cultivation. Mencius reflects a constant concern for "losing the mind and a persistent belief in an innate ability to preserve the mind" (Tu 1998, 63). This idea of "losing the mind" referred to Mencius' conviction that individuals could lose or discard the tendencies of their fallible, impure thoughts and actions and could instead embrace more noble and virtuous thoughts and deeds, thereby living more in harmony with their inborn nature.

A paradox in classical Confucian thought is that while sageliness is in every human, no one—not even Confucius—could claim to be a sage (Tu 1985). Self-realization was the desired outcome of self-cultivation (Berthong and Berthong 2000). Mencius, the second-most influential classical scholar, was completely resolute about the possibility of human perfectibility and self-realization through self-effort (Tu 1998).

Self-realization

Confucian self-realization through self-effort has a spiritual dimension. For example, the Confucian mystical tradition is alluded to in *Mencius* as he refers to a presence in the heart of an actuality greater than itself (Ching 2003). Confucian mysticism unites contemplation and action, the inner and outer, suggesting that external activity is an expression of interior attitudes and one's intentions (ibid.). According to the tradition, the fully realized individual has two defining characteristics. First, he or she is in tune with the way (the natural order of things). Second, he or she has harmonious relations with others (Young and Baker 2004). Confucianism does not deny God's existence.[6]

Confucians believe that with persistent and genuine accumulated effort over time, one will achieve a breakthrough to an "integral comprehension" of things. At this point, one will come to understand situations and events as an undifferentiated "unity."

Interrelationships of situations, events, and affairs will become more apparent (de Bary and Bloom 1999). When one achieves this level of consciousness, he or she will acquire an "empathetic insight" (de Bary 1989) in which all perspectives are considered equally in varied situational contexts.[7] "At this point, 'learning for the sake of oneself'[8] [will]

---

[6] According to Julia Ching, Confucius believed that human beings are accountable to a supreme being: *Analects* III, 13 (1986, 65). He refers to Heaven in this particular passage. (See *Analects* III, 13.) He honors "Heaven" as the supreme source of goodness.

[7] It should be pointed out that while Confucian scholars described this state of "integral consciousness" or "comprehensive understanding" of situations and events (*guantong*), numerous contemporary scholars have also described this integral consciousness and the manner in which this level of consciousness affects individual perceptions. For example, Jean Gebser (1905–1973), a German cultural philosopher, coined the phrase "integral consciousness" (Gebser 1985). He referred to this category-free perception as "waring" (Combs 1985). Martin Heidegger (1889–1976), a German philosopher, referred to this perception as "meditative thinking" (Heidegger 1966). Georg Feurstein (1947–2012), a German Canadian Indologist, referred to this manner of perception as "lucid waking" (Feurstein 1997). Christian philosopher Beatrice Bruteau refers to this state of consciousness as "wholistic consciousness," which represents a "non-dual awareness" (Bruteau 1997, 2001). This "waring," "seeing," "lucid waking," or "non-dual awareness" "requires a presupposed holistic attitude or stance of openness in contrast to an emphasis on parts" (Young and Logsdon 2005, 77). It is an aperspective "seeing"—a nonlinear, more contemplative and intuitive experience of reality (Puhakka 1998). Waring refers to the level of consciousness that causes perceptions to change. When we move to "higher" levels of consciousness, our worldviews change. We essentially become different people or different personalities who hold a new set of values. We are changed from who we were, so to speak. Waring, lucid waking, and meditative thinking are different terms used to describe the same state of consciousness as Gebser's integral consciousness or the Chinese comprehensive understanding of situations.

[8] Confucius subscribed to the concept of learning for the sake of one's own moral development as opposed to learning for the sake of the approval, or certification,

overcome all distinctions between self and others" (ibid., 8). This integral consciousness or comprehensive understanding is referred to as *guantong* (*kuan-t'ung*).[9]

This integral comprehension enabled individuals to experience a comprehensive understanding of events, things, and affairs in an undifferentiated unity or wholeness. This level of consciousness allows individuals to overcome the dichotomy of self and others, inner and outer (de Bary 2004). The concept suggests the idea that understanding consists of "having an insight into the interconnection of all things" (Cua 2003, 633). It represents a holistic ideal, a unifying perspective (ibid.).

Guantong represents one of the highest ideals of individual fulfillment in Song[10] or Neo-Confucian thought and scholarship (de Bary 1991). Table 1 summarizes some of the characteristics of guantong.

Table 1
Some Characteristics of *Guantong*[11]
Integral Consciousness or Comprehensive Understanding

Understanding of situations and events as an undifferentiated "unity"
Recognition of interrelationships of situations, events, and affairs
Empathic insight into situational contexts
Overcoming distinctions between self and others

Learning to be human

The goal of self-cultivation was to learn to be human.

Herbert Fingarette suggested that the primary theme of Confucius' thought is that humans are "born as 'raw material' who must be civilized

---

of others.

[9] For an excellent contemporary comparison of several models of levels of consciousness, in a table format, see Wilber (1999).

[10] Refers to the Song Dynasty (960–1279).

[11] See Young and Logsdon (2005) for a detailed description of integral consciousness, its evolution, and its application in managerial contexts.

by education [learning]" and, as a result, they can become truly human. In order to achieve this transformation, individuals must aim for the Way, and the Way—through its nobility and the nobility of those who pursue it—must attract these individuals (1972, 34–35).

Learning to be human, from Mencius' perspective, means to refine ourselves so that we can become good, beautiful, great, sagely, and spiritual beings (Tu 1985). The Confucian project's objective of learning to be human was expressed when he proposed "learning for the sake of the self" or "learning for one's self" (ibid.). *True learning*, from the Confucian perspective, enhances one's character and practical judgment. This learning, over time, increases one's innate capacity for feeling and understanding. Some measure of a desire to learn and an ability to enjoy "true learning" is inherent in human beings (Gotshalk 1999). However, this love of learning is stronger in some individuals than it is in others (ibid.).

Confucians felt that sincerity of intentions was an essential prerequisite in order to achieve the ultimate transformative goal of self-cultivation. They were not only asking for sincerity but were also seeking an absolute belief in one's spontaneous willingness and ability to practice Confucian principles. Confucians were intent on learning to consistently and spontaneously do the morally correct thing in whatever circumstances they found themselves (Bol 2008). These principles were to be practiced as spontaneous sentiments. They felt that ultimate reality is recognizable and realizable in the moral life of every individual because human nature has the potential to genuinely reflect that ultimate reality (Tu 1989). Theoretically, ordinary individuals have the potential to actualize this unity between Heaven[12] and man in their daily lives and experiences (ibid.). The Neo-Confucian movement contributed significantly to the tradition as it has evolved.

Neo-Confucian influence

Neo-Confucian scholars of the Song Dynasty (960–1279), like the classical scholars before them, felt that advancement in the "outer" realm of

---

[12] Heaven is translated into Chinese as *tian* or *t'ien*. It is one of the oldest Chinese terms for the cosmos and does not refer to an afterlife as it does in Western religions.

political and economic affairs was contingent upon prior development in the "inner" realm of self-cultivation (Gardner 1986). They believed that only good persons could create high-quality reforms and that only virtuous persons could implement those reforms effectively (ibid.).

Song Dynasty Neo-Confucians determined to return to the cultivation of the heart-mind. The heart-mind (*xin* or *hsin*) is the mind generated from both positive and negative emotional influences. Elvin explains that the heart-mind represents "a concept that can be interpreted as the psychological field of force," that impacts and influences the body (1993, 213). It is broader than the intellectual problem-solving mind (*yi*) in that it encompasses both emotions and the intellect. On the other hand, the intellectual problem-solving mind (*yi*) is more narrowly defined. Confucians of the Song Dynasty developed ways to carry out cultivation or rectification of the heart-mind based on study and meditation (Berthong and Berthong 2000). In other words, the goal was to "put right," rectify, or correct the heart-mind.

Unlike the classical period of Confucianism, in which it was felt that sagehood was an unattainable goal or objective, Neo-Confucians believed that sagehood was obtainable. In fact, they believed that it could be achieved through the process of sage learning (Kalton 2004).

Zhu Xi (Chu Hsi) (1130–1200), one of the most influential Neo-Confucian thinkers and a proponent of sage learning, introduced a point of view that combined spiritual and intellectual cultivation (Ching 2003). It was Zhu Xi's perspective that the "end" of the continuous learning process is reached by way of a sudden breakthrough, an experience of inner enlightenment that can occur as the result of a long and arduous process of search and exertion (ibid.).

According to de Bary, Zhu Xi described in his manual for Neo-Confucian practice, *Reflections on Things at Hand*, the state of poise and serenity that could result from Neo-Confucian practice. De Bary describes, "a state of poise and serenity achieved through constant effort and self-discipline in the conduct of life, through which the natural powers of Heaven are manifested effortlessly" (1975, 158). He describes "a process of becoming identified with Heaven, with the reality of a moral and creative universe, so that the virtue of Heaven shines through in one's own life" (ibid.).

Characteristics of Confucian Self-Cultivation

Over the centuries, the process of self-cultivation has evolved to include several inherent characteristics. Some of the characteristics are that the process is holistic, continuous, and cyclical.

Self-cultivation is holistic

Confucians, like all Chinese philosophical perspectives, share a strong commitment to a holistic approach to self-realization (Tu 1985). The process is intended to cultivate the body, mind, and spirit of the practitioner. For example, to Confucians, the physical body provides the context and the resources for ultimate self-transformation. They have a strong commitment to a holistic view of transformation, and they suggest that it is the heart-mind that has the potential to make individuals truly human. According to the scholar Tu Weiming, Confucian self-cultivation typically involves the practice of "mental and physical rejuvenation involving rhythmic bodily movements and breathing techniques" (1985, 171). A significant amount of Confucian literature refers to the value of taking care of one's body as an essential requisite for learning to be human (Tu 1983). According to Tu (1985), such practices represent an "ancient Chinese art."

Self-cultivation is continuous

"Confucians do not believe in fixed personalities. Real personalities are always evolving" (Tu 1985, 178). For instance, it was only after Confucius had reached the age of seventy that he was truly able to say, with confidence, that he could follow his heart's desire without transgressing moral principle (Tu 1998). The Confucian view of adulthood is that of engaging in an active and unending process of learning to be human (ibid.). Tu points out that, from the Confucian perspective, "even the mature person does not cease to learn" because developing our innate human qualities requires constant refinement (1983, 59). This process of learning to be human implies a continual spiritual self-transformation (Tu 1998). Confucians have always considered the process of "*becoming humane* as a process of spiritual growth" (Ching 1986b, 71).

Self-cultivation is cyclical

While the Confucian perception of adulthood is that of engaging in an active and unending process of learning to be human, self-cultivation is best described as a cyclical journey (Tu 1998). Podgorski (1985) suggested that the process of self-cultivation resembles both an outward and an inward journey. As such, the sojourn is characterized by a continuous cycle of disciplined inner and outer probing, self-reflection, and necessary self-correction. Kalton (2004) describes this approach as an alternation between absolute quiet (quiescence) and activity. This process of Confucian self-cultivation can also be thought of as a "circular movement" from the mind to things and events, and back to the mind (Ching 2000, 2003). This circular movement is not undertaken for its own sake but rather to act properly, to understand, and to embark upon moral behavior (Ching 1986b). Cyclical Confucian self-cultivation typically takes place both alone and in the company of others. Some of the characteristics of Confucian self-cultivation are summarized in Table 2.

Table 2
Some Characteristics of Confucian Self-Cultivation

Holistic, cultivates	Body Mind (heart-mind, *xin* or *hsin*) Spirit
Ongoing	Personalities always evolving Unceasing spiritual transformation
Cyclical	Cyclical learning to be human Outward and inward journey (outer and inner probing) Self-reflection, self-correction Alternating quiet and activity Circular—mind, things and events, mind

CHAPTER 2

Self-Cultivation as a Communal Act

"A Confucianist always carries out his moral self-cultivation in the social context" (Tu 1998, 12). Mencius suggested that the ideal self-transformation process was not a solitary quest for one's inner spirituality but was instead a communal act (Tu 1985). Tu (1989) explains that self-cultivation is not merely a remote search for interior spirituality but also represents a persistent attempt at interpersonal communication. Self-cultivation therefore extends beyond one's self.

Lü Liuliang (Lü Liu-liang) (1629–1683) suggested that through communication with others, one is able to engage in the mutual encouragement and fulfillment of one another's humanity (de Bary 1991). Therefore, the development of one's humanity frequently occurs in group settings.

When two or more individuals engage in self-cultivation together, this is referred to as a "communal act" (Tu 1989, 96). Confucians believe that in order to morally and spiritually transform one's self, interaction with like-minded individuals is essential (Tu 1989). This is why dialogue is an essential feature of Confucian self-cultivation. It serves as a mechanism that provides individuals with a venue for speaking "passionately without animosity" (Angle 2009, 173), and thereby contributes to their growth and development. Dialogue in learning communities enables participants to engage in questioning and to express openness, humility, clarity, and so forth in a common quest for personal development (Angle 2009).

From the Confucian perspective, an individual is expected to validate his or her personal transformational journey by exhibiting and demonstrating harmonious relationships with others. Confucians feel that unless one cultivates oneself in the context of human relatedness, the depth of one's spiritual journey is immaterial, and hence one's claim to spiritual progress is false (Tu 1998). A fiduciary community is one in which the moral well-being of each member is the personal concern of everyone (Tu 1985). It represents a community, or a society, of mutual trust rather than a mere aggregation of individuals. "In such a society, the goal of the people is not only to live in peace but also to aid each other in moral development as they cultivate their own personal characters" (Tu 1989, 86). In a fiduciary community, one becomes fully human within the context of a community (Tu 1989).

Such societies also provide a source of motivation for individuals to improve themselves (Angle 2009). "Disinterested fellowship, dedicated to moral growth, is far superior to relationships dictated by need" (Tu 1985, 56). For this reason, Confucian self-cultivation is typically carried out as an intentional communal act (Tu 1985).

Stated differently, Berthong and Berthong (2000) suggest that there are both vertical and horizontal dimensions of self-cultivation. The vertical aspect involves cultivating oneself to be in tune with the Way (*Dao*).[13] The horizontal aspect involves the cultivation of harmonious and respectful relations with other people.

Vertical and Horizontal Aspects of Self-Cultivation

From the perspective of Confucius, there was a polarity within the concept of sagehood. In fact, to be a sage implied that one had not only achieved moral perfection but had also succeeded in serving the people. Achieving moral perfection represented an inner or vertical aspect of self-cultivation, while serving the people represented an outer or horizontal aspect, which in turn led to the ordering of society (Gardner 1990).

The vertical and horizontal aspects of self-cultivation are manifested in the tension between the two important classical Confucian concepts of *ren* (*jen*) and *li*. There is an implicit tension between these concepts.

---

[13] *Dao* or *Tao* can be translated as the Way, a path, a way of proper conduct … a matrix of all things and events of the cosmos (Tu and Tucker 2004, 509).

Ren (jen)

Perhaps the most important concept of classical Confucianism is *ren* (goodness, humanity, humaneness).[14] *Ren* is the central virtue of Confucianism and the most important characteristic of the ideal or exemplary person (*junzi/chün-tzu*).[15] Prior to Confucius, *ren* represented the particular virtue that distinguished a gentleman (*junzi*) from his inferiors. However, Confucius transformed the concept "into a universal virtue" that exemplified the sage (Ching 1986b, 65). *Ren* is the predominant virtue in the teachings of Confucius, and is considered as such by generations of subsequent Confucians and contemporary or New Confucian scholars (Taylor 2005, 310).[16] Confucius characterized *ren* as love for others, personal integrity, and altruism (Ching 1986b, 65). It is the "warm and compassionate concern that extends, in an organic fashion, to all related and relevant aspects of one's context" (Angle 2009, 78). Confucius felt that this virtue was accessible, could be learned, and, once learned, engendered a "profound sense of the fulfillment of being human" (Taylor 2005, 312).

Ren is basically linked with the self-reviving, self-perfecting, and self-fulfilling process of an individual (Tu 1998). It is the manifestation of pure, untarnished human nature in accordance with the requirements of morality (Fischer-Schreiber, Ehrhard, Friedrichs, Diener 1994). Zhu Xi (1130–1200), the famous Neo-Confucian scholar who will be discussed later, described *ren* as "the character of man's mind and the principle of love" (Chan 1963, 591).[17] *Ren* was believed to be a natural quality found

---

[14] *Ren* or *jen* can be translated as humaneness, humanity, human-relatedness, benevolence, or love. It is the first of the Confucian virtues (Tu and Tucker 2004, 510).

[15] Also translated as the profound person (Tu 1989) or superior person (e.g., Chan 1963).

[16] Even today, in the writings of contemporary Confucians, *ren* remains "the single thread" that runs through all Confucian philosophy (Taylor 2005, 313).

[17] In Zhu Xi's *Treatise on Ren,* he stated, "If we can truly practice love and preserve it, then we have in it the spring of all virtues and the root of all good deeds" (Chan 1963, 594). Zhu Xi felt that the "substance" of *ren* is the character of the mind, while

within every individual. It includes wisdom, propriety, and righteousness (ibid., 597).

Zhu Xi, the Neo-Confucian synthesizer of Confucian ideas, stated that "*Ren* is the principle of love, and impartiality is the principle of *ren*. Therefore, if there is impartiality, there is *ren*, and if there is *ren* there is love" (ibid., 633). Further, Chan quotes Zhu Xi as stating, "Impartiality, altruism, and love are all descriptions of *ren*. Impartiality is antecedent to *ren*, altruism and love are subsequent. This is so because impartiality makes *ren* possible, and *ren* makes love and altruism possible" (ibid.).

Enhancing *ren* develops an internal state of mental and emotional equilibrium within the Confucian practitioner. This developed state of equilibrium, also referred to as centrality, represents a "state of mind wherein one is absolutely unperturbed by outside forces" (Tu 1989, 20). Bol asserts that "equilibrium describes an unstirred and unstimulated" mental and emotional state (2008, 195). Enhancing one's *ren* develops one's centrality or equilibrium.

On the other hand, in classical Confucianism, *li* is the external manifestation of an individual's *ren*. Enhancing *li* leads to increased harmony in one's relationships with others.

Li

Li is conceptualized in two important but distinct ways.[18] The first is the classical rendering of the term. The second is the Neo-Confucian use of the term, which will be discussed in depth later.

Historically, the classical understanding of the term can be traced from the Shang Dynasty (circa 1600 BCE–circa 1045 BCE)[19] through the twentieth century (Taylor 2005, 367). The concept was one of great importance to Confucius, as well as to later Confucian scholars (ibid.).

---

the "function" of *ren* is the principle of love (ibid.). *Ren* represents universal nature and is within every individual.

[18] Actually three unique Chinese characters are translated as *li*. The classical and Neo-Confucian interpretations are discussed here. A third definition is "to establish, set up, to make firm (in virtue and conduct)" (Tu and Tucker 2004, 510).

[19] The Shang Dynasty is also referred to as the Yin Dynasty.

From this perspective, *li* is defined as ritual propriety, etiquette, or rules of proper behavior. Here, *li* refers to the rules that govern proper social relationships. It refers to the conventions governing human relationships, including ceremonies, and how to act in a given situation.

Mencius viewed *li* as a part of the basic moral character of humankind.[20] It serves as a means of experiencing one's inherent benevolence (*ren*) (Fischer-Schreiber, Ehrhard, Friedrichs, Diener 1994) and can be seen as the externalization of *ren* in a specific social circumstance (Tu 1998).

Ren and *li*

Taken together, these concepts represent a dichotomy of "inner" versus "outer" (ibid., 18), in which *ren* represents the vertical aspect of Confucian inner development and *li* represents the horizontal (external), relational dimension of Confucian progress. *Li* is dependent upon the extent to which one's *ren* is developed or cultivated. Confucius believed that one's inner, and therefore implicitly outer, moral and spiritual development could be facilitated through the process of personal learning.[21]

Confucian spirituality cultivates one's "inner" spirituality, or "inner sageliness," as well as one's "outer kingliness." Confucian practice is intended to develop and unite "a life of contemplation and a life of activity" (Ching 1986, 80). Cultivating one's equilibrium, or centrality, as well as one's harmony with others can be undertaken through an unceasing process of learning (Tu 1989).

---

[20] Mencius considered *li* to be one of the Four Beginnings, which were also referred to by Confucius. However, Mencius believed that the Four Beginnings of humaneness, righteousness or rightness, propriety or rites (*li*), and wisdom are inherent in human nature.

[21] For example, the first chapter of the *Analects* of Confucius begins as follows: "To learn, and then, in its due season, put what you have learned into practice—isn't that still a great pleasure?" (Hinton 1998a, 3).

CHAPTER 3

Confucian Learning

Motivation for Learning

Confucian learning is motivated by a universal, deep-seated, human desire to improve one's own moral and spiritual understanding and experience. Confucius suggested that when one's heart becomes set on learning, such learning implies a sense of lifelong evolution, development, and growth. Therefore, historically, Confucians made a distinction between two types of learning: (1) learning for the sake of one's own moral and spiritual development, and (2) learning for the sake of others and winning their approval, recognition, or acclaim. Confucian practice is different from other self-help practices in the sense that Confucian self-development represents a lifelong dedication, which compels an unending process of learning (Tu 1985). Confucian students took responsibility for their own individual spiritual practice through methodical study (Keenan 2011). This orderly study leads to the acquisition of knowledge.

Confucian knowledge

From the perspective of the "Three Teachings" (Daoism, Confucianism, and Chan Buddhism) of classical China, knowledge represents an understanding of one's mental state and an appreciation of one's inner feelings (Tu 1985). Learning, therefore, implies the process of getting in touch with and realizing the status or knowledge of one's mental state and inner feelings. So "learning motivated by reasons other than self-knowledge— such as fame, position and wealth—cannot be considered true learning" (ibid., 56). True learning accumulates self-knowledge and brings philo-sophical insight into the human condition.

Confucius was well known for teaching anyone who desired to learn and, consequently, improve him or herself (Berthong and Berthong 2000). Specifically, Confucian learning was for the sake of one's self, for one's own moral, ethical, and spiritual development. It was learning for those who were intent on acquiring the self-knowledge required to become more human.

Confucians believe that learning begins with one's self, which can be conceived of as the center of an ever-expanding circle of human rela-tionships. The self, which is also influenced by this ever-expanding circle of relationships, is therefore considered an open system,[22] ever changing over time through self-cultivation and learning (Tu 1985).

Neo-Confucian Impact on Learning

Neo-Confucians introduced a new meaning for the term *li*. While classi-cal Confucians saw the term to mean ritual propriety, etiquette, or rules of proper behavior, Neo-Confucians accepted this classical definition and then added another dimension to the term. They used the expression to also mean "rational principle," "law," or "coherence."

Neo-Confucian philosophy emerged as a result of the impact of several social factors (Huang 1999). The movement arose as a reaction against foreign invasions from the north during the Song Dynasty (960–1279). In addition, the movement was a backlash against the prevalence of Buddhist philosophy. It was also influenced by Daoism (ibid.). The Neo-Confucians, who emerged during the Song Dynasty, felt a need to add to their philosophy something of the spiritual depth that had made Buddhism (especially Chan or Zen Buddhism) so compelling within the Chinese culture.[23]

---

[22] An "open system" is one that influences and is influenced by its environments, and a "closed system" functions impervious to its situational environments.

[23] Tu (1986) points out that Neo-Confucianism, while it initially emerged during the Song (960–1279) and Ming (1368–1643) dynasties, was also significantly influential during the Jin (Jurchen) Dynasty (1115–1234) of northern China, as well as the Yuan (1271–1368) and Qing (1644–1912) dynasties. Additionally, Neo-Confucianism

Daoist and Buddhist ideas significantly influenced the Song Confucian vocabulary of self-cultivation (Tu 1993). The concept of *li*, as expressed by the Neo-Confucians, resembles the Buddhist notion of *li*. However, the Neo-Confucian concept was said to have had its origin in the *Yi Jing* (*I Ching*, or the *Book of Changes*), a classic Chinese text. They expanded Confucian self-cultivation to emphasize Chan meditation and the practice of the arts (Hinton 1998b). Learning, in the Neo-Confucian sense, requires continuous effort and commitment.[24]

The aim of Neo-Confucian learning

Neo-Confucians believed that one purpose or objective of learning was to cultivate an awareness of the coherence in things, events, and one's self (Bol 2008). Further, they felt that because there is always an underlying or latent coherence in affairs and events, in theory there must always be an appropriate coherent response to all affairs and events (ibid.). The outcome of successful Neo-Confucian learning was an individual capable of instinctively seeing or intuiting the potential harmonious patterns in daily life (ibid.).

The attainability of sagehood

From the Neo-Confucian perspective, sagehood was an achievable objective. Zhou Dunyi (Chou Tun-i) (1017–1073), one of the founding fathers of the Neo-Confucian movement, wrote a chapter titled "Sage Learning," in which he asked, "Can sagehood be learned?" Subsequently within his chapter, he answered with an emphatic yes (Kalton 2004). Similarly, early Neo-Confucian thinkers, such as the Cheng brothers, were explicit that

---

significantly influenced the Yi or Chosön (1392–1910) Dynasty of Korea, the Tokugawa period in Japan (1600–1867), and the Le (1428–1789) Dynasty of Vietnam (Tu 1986).

[24] Neo-Confucian synthesizer Zhu Xi stated that, "Although there may not seem to be substantial progress, nevertheless after a long period of accumulation, without knowing it one will be saturated [with principle] and achieve an extensive harmony and penetration. Truly, one cannot succeed if one wants to hurry" (Chan 1963, 611).

"sagehood could be studied and attained" (Angle 2009, 17). For them, sages are spontaneous, moral, and flexible (i.e., less tied to a single perspective), and edify others (Angle 2009).[25] Unlike classical Confucians, who suggested that attaining sagehood was an improbable objective, Neo-Confucians firmly believed that sagehood was indeed attainable (ibid.).

Ching (2000) states that the sage is an individual who has liberated him or herself from the obstacles imposed by desires or passions on his or her vital energy or *qi* (*chi*). When these hindrances are removed, his or her Heavenly principle (*tianli*) becomes manifest. *Tianli* can be considered a moral force present within all individuals; it reflects both transcendence and immanence[26] (Ching 2000). *Tianli* is another name for the Great Ultimate present within each individual (ibid.).[27, 28]

The examination of *li*

Neo-Confucians engaged in sage learning, or learning to become a sage, by examining *li* (Kalton 2004). The term *li* (coherence) is a difficult expression that lies at the center of Neo-Confucian philosophy. The term is also frequently translated as "principle." Angle defined Neo-Confucian *li* as "the valuable, intelligible way that things fit together" (2009, 32).[29]

---

[25] Jean Gebser (1905–1973), a German cultural philosopher, later referred to this lack of rigid situational perspective as being "aperspective" in one's thinking and worldview (1985).

[26] In other words, Heavenly principle (*tianli*) transcends and is also within the universe.

[27] Ching explains, "The sage is the person who is able to rid himself [or herself] of the impediments imposed by *qi* through human desires or passions and so make manifest his [or her] heavenly principle ..." (2000, 113).

[28] The Great Ultimate is frequently translated "Supreme Ultimate" (e.g., Zang 2002). The Great Ultimate or Supreme Ultimate is referred to as *Taiji* in Chinese. During the Song Dynasty, Zhu Xi (1130–1200) took the Great Ultimate to be the highest principle, one that subsumed all other principles (Zang 2002, 186). Zhu felt that this principle was supreme in both cosmic and moral terms (ibid.).

[29] Zhang Dainian discusses how the concept of *li* evolved from the Pre-Qin Era (2,100–221 BCE) through the Song Dynasty (960–1279) to the Ming-Qing Period

He quotes Zhu Xi, who explained that "each coherence has ordered elements and distinct segments" (ibid.). Hence, we see that multiple and hierarchical levels of coherence can overlap or nest within each other (Angle 2009).[30] Each *li* (principle, coherence, or focus) can also be viewed as holographic in the sense that it contains within it the entire extensive field.[31] Ames and Hall (2001) refer to this changing focus/field perspective as pervasive in traditional Chinese philosophy. As a result of its multiple and hierarchical levels, *li* can be examined indefinitely by making finer and finer distinctions among many hierarchical levels (Graham 1992). Finally, all Neo-Confucian scholars believed that there is one maximal or ultimate coherence (*tianli*[32] or universal coherence) that encompasses everything (Angle 2009).

Coherence, "the valuable and intelligible way that things fit together" (ibid., 32), can be characterized in numerous ways (ibid., 67). However, the essential idea for sage learning is the search for and discovery of a harmonious, organic unity within and among things and events. While each thing or event is different, harmony involves ensuring that each element and hierarchical sub-element receives its due weight and consideration at the appropriate time and/or place. Therefore, harmony is the discovery and achievement of coherence (Angle 2009). Sages "maximize harmonious possibilities within any given situation" (ibid., 99).[33] Some of the characteristics of Neo-Confucian *li* are listed in Table 3 below.

(1368–1911) (Zhang 2002).

[30] For example, nature and natural phenomena provide ubiquitous examples of hierarchical manifestations of Neo-Confucian *li*.

[31] For an in-depth discussion of holonomic processes and the holographic concept, see *The Holographic Paradigm and Other Paradoxes* (1985), edited by Ken Wilber, Boston: Shambhala.

[32] *Tianli* is also translated as Heavenly principle, ultimate principle, or norm of the good or perfect (Tu and Tucker 2004).

[33] Wang Yangming as cited by Prof. Warren G. Frisina of Hofstra University (Frisina 2002, 85).

Table 3
Some Characteristics of Neo-Confucian *Li*

Li—various translations: rational principle, law, coherence, pattern	
Characteristics:	Each *li*: • has its ordered elements and distinct segments • has multiple and/or hierarchical levels • can have multiple and hierarchical levels that can overlap or nest within each other. • can be examined indefinitely by making finer and finer distinctions among multiple and hierarchical levels.
Examining *li*	Essential idea—the search for and discovery of a harmonious, organic unity among things and events. Harmony ensures that each element and hierarchical subelement receives its due weight and consideration at the appropriate time and/or place.
There is one maximal or ultimate "*li*" (*tianli*) that encompasses everything. *Tianli* is translated as Heavenly principle or ultimate principle.	

Coherence (*li*) and a mental state of unity

Neo-Confucians emphasized the process of learning as a means of experiencing and maintaining a mental state of unity (Bol 2008). A state of mental unity is achieved when an individual experiences that all *li* are one *li*, which can also be thought of as a state of coherence. This status is achieved the moment an individual sees how everything he or she understands is connected together in a seamless whole, as if on a single thread. It is the moment when the *li* (coherence) within an individual's mind recognizes, and hence resonates with, the *li* in things and events (ibid.). Neo-Confucians believed that a mental state of unity could be achieved, over a long period of time, by engaging in the process of learning.[34]

---

[34] During the Song Dynasty (960–1279) the image of one body was emphasized. For example, Cheng Hao, one of the Cheng brothers, believed that the highest state

Finding the "lost mind"

In the ordinary state of affairs, we have a deep-seated alienation from our original nature (Tu 1998). The way of learning is the process of rediscovering our original nature or lost mind, and finding the lost mind allows the four germinations, or Four Beginnings, to blossom. These four germinations—properties that reside deeply within all humans—are humanity, righteousness, propriety, and wisdom; they are not learned from the outside.[35] We originally have them within ourselves (Tu 1998, 64, 67). Finding the lost mind, our original nature, allows the four germinations to emerge.

Learning in the tradition of Confucian education includes intellectual growth and development, ethical growth and development, and physical development. It incorporates learning within the spheres of both mind and body (Tu 1998). In the Confucian tradition, learning includes cognitive and affective elements. Cognitive learning occurs as "individuals knowingly increase their levels of understanding" and their knowledge base of factual information (Young and Corzine 2004, 81). Affective learning, or breakthroughs, occurs as individuals "move to more sophisticated levels of emotional awareness and understanding" (ibid.).

Neo-Confucians believed that when practiced correctly, true learning could not only make the individual student more morally perfect but that it also had the potential to transform society as a whole, making it less vulnerable to "barbarian" peoples and "heterodox" (i.e., unusual) philosophies, religions, and beliefs (Gardner 1990). The most important document to singularly elaborate on the process of learning within the Confucian tradition is the *Great Learning,* one of the most influential documents to impact the learning process within the Confucian tradition.

---

of human life was to realize the unity of heaven, earth, and the myriad things. This perspective of the unity of heaven and human beings was prominent within Neo-Confucian philosophy (Zhang 2002, 268–269).

[35] The four germinations, also referred to as the Four Beginnings, were discussed by Mencius and reflect his belief in a natural human tendency toward the sympathetic responsiveness to others (Bloom 1999).

The Principal Teachings of the *Great Learning*[36]

According to Zhu Xi (1130–1200), the *Great Learning* was transmitted by Zengzi (Tseng Tzu) (505 BCE–436 BCE), a disciple of Confucius. Zengzi transmitted the text to his disciples, who in turn recorded the ideas of their teacher (Gardner 1986). According to Chan (1963), the *Great Learning* neatly summarizes the Confucian educational, moral, and political programs. It, along with Zhu Xi's additional commentary, became the standard for self-cultivation of most subsequent Neo-Confucians (Keenan 2011).[37]

Historically, the Cheng brothers, Cheng Hao (1032–1085) and Cheng Yi (1033–1107), from Honan Province did more to enhance the status of the *Great Learning* within the Confucian canon than any scholar before Zhu Xi. Although Zhu Xi never heard the teachings of either of the Cheng brothers directly, he nevertheless was able to study their teachings by means of their students' writings (Gardner 1986). With the Cheng brothers, the *Great Learning* became essential reading for all who sought self-perfection, and the text became the foundation of a Neo-Confucian education (ibid.).

The text discusses recommendations for adult education, for individuals intent on increasing their own moral understanding and true learning. It sets forth what have been referred to as the "three items" or "three principles." These three principles can be conceived as outcomes achieved by engaging in eight learning steps, or processes. Two translations of the three outcome items that can be realized, according to the *Great Learning*, are as follows:

1. "manifesting the clear character of man" (Chan 1963)

   "keeping the inborn luminous Virtue unobscured" (Gardner 1986)

---

[36] In 1313, during the Yuan (Mongol) Dynasty (1260–1368), the *Great Learning*—along with the *Analects*, the *Mencius*, and the *Doctrine of the Mean*—became the "Four Books," which were the basis of the civil service examinations for the next six hundred years, until 1905.

[37] The leading Confucians in China, as well as in Chosŏn-era (or Yi Dynasty) Korea (1392–1910) and Tokugawa Japan (1603–1868), promoted the essential importance of the *Great Learning* in the process of self-cultivation (Keenan 2011).

2. "loving the people (Chan 1963)
    "renewing the people" (Gardner 1986)

3. "abiding in the highest good" (Chan 1963)
    "coming to rest in perfect goodness" (Gardner 1986)

Two translations of the eight learning steps that enable individuals to bring into fruition the above listed outcomes are as follows:[38]

1. "the investigation of things" (Chan 1963)
    "apprehending the principle in things" (Gardner 1986)

This activity seeks to understand broadly why both moral and natural principles function they way they do.[39]

2. "extension of knowledge" (Chan 1963)
    "extending knowledge" (Gardner 1986)

The second process involves the internalization, in one's heart-mind, of the moral and physical principles discovered in the first step.[40]

3. "sincerity of the will" (Chan 1963)
    "making the thoughts true" (Gardner 1986)

This step insists on honesty and self-scrutiny regarding what one is doing and why.[41]

4. "rectification of the mind" (Chan 1963)
    "setting the mind right" (Gardner 1986)

---

[38] Barry C. Keenan's interpretation of Zhu Xi's understanding of each process is presented after each step (2011, 38–72).

[39] This process is referred to as *gewu* or *ko-wu*.

[40] Inner mental attentiveness, *jing* (*ching*), is essential for carrying out this step.

[41] This process requires sincere self-scrutiny of one's attitude, motives, and actions.

The mind can be rectified by either (a) remaining in control of one's thoughts and willpower by focusing and refocusing on the task at hand, or (b) preventing emotions from distorting one's thoughts; and curbing fleeting passions, thereby leading to better judgment.

5. "cultivation of personal life" (Chan 1963)
    "cultivating the person" (Gardner 1986)

In this step, one attempts to sustain his or her honest intentions and correct actions. One endeavors to sustain consistent moral actions and attitudes that would distinguish a truly humane person.

6. "regulation of the family" (Chan 1963)
    "establishing harmony in the household" (Gardner 1986)

This process suggests that once individuals understand how to be humane to people, they will extend these attitudes and behaviors to loving all things because extending such attitudes and behaviors to all things is similar in kind.[42]

7. "governing the state well" (Chan 1963)
    "national order" (Gardner 1986)

This step suggests that the extended family can serve as a natural basis for social and political order.

8. "world peace" (Chan 1963)
    "bringing tranquility to the empire" (Gardner 1986)

In this final step, the tranquility of the nation depends on the quality of humane character emanating from its government.

The *Great Learning* discusses the application of the doctrine of

---

[42] This methodology of generalizing to a higher conceptual level is referred to as *inferring by analogy.*

humanity (*ren* or *jen*). It promotes action on the part of the individual toward the ultimate goal of self-cultivation through the "expansion of knowledge and the investigation of things" (*Great Learning,* Wikipedia 2009). Some of the most important concepts mentioned in the *Great Learning* are as follows:

- Achieving a state of balance and refining one's moral self so that it is a reflection of the *Dao* (Way).
- Ample rest and reflection so that one achieves peace of mind. When individuals are calm and reflective, the Way will be revealed to them.
- Setting priorities and knowing what is important is essential in one's quest for moral refinement, for it allows one to focus on that which is of the greatest importance and that which is in line with the Way as outlined in Confucian teachings.
- One must bring one's affairs and relationships into order and harmony. If one hopes to attain order in the state, one must first get his/her own family and personal life in order through self-cultivation, the expansion of one's knowledge, and the investigation of things.
- Each and every person is capable of learning and self-cultivation, regardless of social, economic, or political status. This, in turn, means that success in learning is the result of the individual's effort as opposed to an inability to learn.
- One must treat education as an intricate and interrelated system where one must strive for balance. No one aspect of learning is isolated from the other, and failure to cultivate a single aspect of one's learning will lead to the failure of learning as a whole. (Wikipedia 2009)

The *Great Learning* links individual action in the form of self-cultivation with higher goals, such as ultimate world peace, as well as linking together the spiritual and material well-being of individuals and society (ibid.). It suggests that the sociopolitical order is dependent on the moral state of those living within that order (Gardner 1990).

An important concept introduced in the *Great Learning* is the idea of "the investigation of things." A major controversy has been to define and operationalize this idea. For instance, which things are to be investigated, and how they should be investigated, has been one of the key questions of Chinese philosophy (*Great Learning*, Wikipedia 2009).

CHAPTER 4

The Investigation of Things

The precept expressed in the *Great Learning,* which came to be known as *Daoxue (Ta-hsueh)* or Learning of the Way, was that knowledge may be extended through the investigation of things *(gewu) (ko-wu).* According to the Neo-Confucian perspective, we examine things in order to discover their ultimate principles and meanings (Berthong and Berthong 2000). Individuals look for the lessons or principles found in the investigation of phenomena.

The Cheng brothers, Hao and Yi, each had a significant influence on Neo-Confucian learning and the concept of self-cultivation. However, while Cheng Hao emphasized internal self-cultivation, his brother Cheng Yi suggested that one should engage in internal self-cultivation and the external extension of knowledge at the same time (Chan 1963). While Cheng Hao said little about the investigation of things, Cheng Yi made it a key concept within his philosophical system (ibid.). He concluded that the quality of moral governance of the state, family, and individual depends fundamentally on the individual's insight into principle, or *li* (Graham 1992).

Cheng Yi and Learning of the Way (*Daoxue* or *Tao-hsueh*)

Cheng Yi (Ch'eng I) (1033–1107) initiated the movement that led to the Learning of the Way, which became the most important intellectual force during the Southern Song Period (1127–1279) (Bol 1992). He and his brother referred to their method of spiritual and moral development as *Daoxue,* or Learning of the Way (ibid.).

Cheng Yi and *qi* (*chi*)

Neo-Confucians in particular felt that principle (*li*) and vital energy (*qi*) were everywhere and always conjoined, or united, in the manifestation of any thing or event (Berthong and Berthong 2000). *Qi* is the psychophysical substance that constitutes all existing phenomena, including "all the phases of matter, energy, mind (*xin* or *hsin*)" and the various forms of spirit (*shen*) (Adler 2004, 122). Self-cultivation through moral learning clarifies *qi*. During this *qi* clarification process, *tianli*, or Heavenly principle, begins to shine through one's material nature.

The Cheng brothers studied under Zhou Dunyi (Chou Tun-i) (1017–1073) as well as their uncle Zhang Zai (Chang Tsai) (1020–1077). Like Confucius, Zhang Zai stressed the moral imperative for learning. However, he emphasized that the process of learning represents a psychospiritual transformation that refines and clarifies one's *qi* (Adler 2004). Adler further states that, according to Zhang Zai, *qi* covers the entire spectrum of body, mind, and spirit. He believed that *qi*, in its rarefied state, is invisible and insubstantial. When it condenses, it becomes solid or liquid.

Zhu Xi, relying on the previous work of Zhang Zai and the Cheng brothers, felt that *li* (coherence or principle) needs *qi* for its existence (Kim 2000). "For Zhu Xi, *qi* provides a place of *li* to be 'settled in,' 'attached,' 'adhered to,' or to 'stand on'" (ibid., 37). Zhu felt that "There is principle [*li*] before there can be material force [*qi*]. But it is only when there is material force [*qi*] that principle [*li*] finds a place to settle" (Chan 1963, 637).

Cheng Yi believed that the status or condition of one's vital energy, or *qi*, had a deterministic effect on one's moral and spiritual development. He also felt that an individual's *qi* could be improved by nurturing one's mind and thoughts with moral principles. This belief reflected the earlier premise of Mencius, who felt that human nature was intrinsically good and that an individual's *qi* could be improved (Bol 1992).

Cheng Yi felt that individuals who cultivate themselves through learning, regardless of whether their *qi* was clear or turbid, could attain goodness and thus reestablish their original nature. Further, the reason individuals do not know good is because their *qi* obscures and blocks it.

Therefore, when individuals engage in evil actions and activities, such actions can be traced to their cloudy or turbid *qi*. He felt that regardless of the quality of an individual's *qi*, one has the capacity to clarify his or her *qi* and become conscious or aware of *li* (coherence or principle) (Bol 1992).

The Learning of the Way and *qi*

Prior to the emergence of the Neo-Confucians, Mencius perceived a unity between the mind and the body (Bloom 1985). He intuited "a necessary connection between maintaining a sense of moral balance and nourishing [one's] psychophysical energy or *chi* [*qi*]" (ibid., 303).

Later, Neo-Confucians argued that when one's individual *qi* is properly nourished, the continuity of the individual with a larger reality becomes evident (ibid.). When individuals honor this connection between themselves, all living things, and this larger reality, their well-being is enhanced (ibid.).

The specific connection between Learning of the Way and *qi* rests on the fact that *qi* covers the entire spectrum of the body, mind, and spirit (Adler 2004). The *qi* that constitutes the mind is pure and invisible and circulates throughout the body. This *qi* resides primarily in the heart-mind (*xin* or *hsin*).[43] The process of learning, according to the Cheng-Zhu School,[44] is a process of psychospiritual transformation that refines and clarifies one's *qi* (ibid.).

Zhu Xi suggested that "the learning of the Sages is to base one's mind on fully investigating principles, and to accord or conform with principle by responding to things" (ibid., 133). Adler explains this resonance of mind *qi* with external things as follows:

> Knowledge of a particular principle, then, is the ordering
> or conforming of mind-*qi* (*chi*) to that principle, so that

---

[43] Recall that in chapter 1 it says the heart-mind represents "a concept that can be interpreted as the psychological field of force" that impacts and influences the body (Elvin 1993, 213).

[44] The Cheng-Zhu School of Neo-Confucian thought is based primarily on the ideas of the Cheng brothers and Zhu Xi.

> when a principle is known it is concretely embodied by
> the mind. That is, when mind penetrates and responds
> (or conforms) to the order or principle of a thing, the
> mind itself is transformed in the process. (ibid.)

This course of action describes how the process of learning transforms mind-*qi*.

Shen (spirit) in this context represents the finest free-flowing *qi*, which has the capacity for unlimited responsiveness and penetration of all things. *Shen* is the capacity to conform, respond, or resonate with the principle (*li*) of all things. The potential to be *shen* is in all *qi*; however, in humans, *shen* functions most prominently in the mind of the sage (Adler 2004, 134).

Cheng Yi, *gewu*, and *li*

Cheng Yi's major philosophical accomplishment was to describe the ways in which individuals could gain moral knowledge. He stated, "In all activities there are principles; to arrive at principles is *gewu*" (Graham 1992, 74). Here, *gewu* is translated as "the investigation of things." Cheng explained how one gains moral knowledge by making *li* (coherence or pattern) the core of one's philosophy (Bol 1992). Bol cites the following Cheng quote regarding his premise:

> When you have fully realized the pattern (coherence)
> of a thing, then, gradually, it will be possible to fully
> reach all things under heaven; they are a single pattern
> (coherence). (1992, 317)

Cheng stated,

> A thing is an event. If the principles (coherence) un-
> derlying the event are investigated to the utmost, there
> all principles (coherence) will be understood. (Chan
> 1963, 552)

In other words, Cheng held to the idea that all patterns, or coherence, are one. The *li* of vastly different things and affairs is ultimately one *li*. His saying "'Principle is one but its manifestations are many' has become one of the most celebrated philosophical statements in China" (Chan 1963, 544). Keenan explains Cheng Yi's philosophical premise this way: "The pattern, or web, of principles underlying things and events constitutes a coherent and orderly whole, and that order in the cosmos is shared because all things have principles; while principle is one, its manifestations are many" (2011, 11). This statement also summarizes Neo-Confucian metaphysics.

The concept that *li* represented patterns that were in fact a single pattern occurring in many things had been accepted in Tang (618–907) and Northern Song (960–1127)[45] culture prior to Cheng Yi (Bol 1992, 318). However, Cheng Yi was the first philosopher to make this idea the core of his philosophy (Bol 1992).

Since Zhu Xi, the students of Cheng Yi have divided the process of uniting the self and *li* (coherence or principle) into two parts; internal cultivation and external cultivation. Both facets of this process, of uniting the self and *li*, are discussed next.

Internal cultivation

The internal aspect of Learning of the Way (*Daoxue*) calls for arriving at a psychophysical state of *jing* (which is not translatable to a single word or concept). Cheng Yi felt that during the internal aspect of self-cultivation, one is concerned with maintaining or preserving the unity of the mind. Graham explains Cheng Yi's perspective on how to preserve this unity of the mind:

> How does one preserve this unity when the mind is active? In activity the mind tends to become confused, with unconnected thoughts getting in each other's way; its unity is maintained by attending to only one thing

---

[45] The Northern Song Dynasty reigned from 960 to 1127. Cheng Yi (1033–1107) lived during this dynasty. The Southern Song Dynasty reign was from 1127 to 1279. Hence, the total number of years of Song reign was from 960 to 1279.

at a time and fully orienting oneself towards it, without
being distracted by anything else. (1992, 68)

This psychological state is referred to as *jing*.

Jing has been translated as several different expressions, including
inner mental attentiveness, composure, reverence, and seriousness. By
arriving at a state of *jing*, mental activity resonates with *li*, one's will
controls one's *qi*, pure *qi* comes into being, and the individual moves into
a state of goodness (Bol 1992).

Cheng Yi explained the difference between moral and immoral behaviors, actions, and attitudes as follows. Since Mencius first suggested
that true human nature is basically good, the effect of disciplining and
training is to refine one's *qi* to a perfect transparency. When this is
achieved, the *li* from Heaven (*tianli*) will show through in one's life,
actions, and morals, and it becomes effortless to live in accordance with
one's true nature (Graham 1985). However, the density of one's *qi* varies
from person to person. When one's *qi* is turbid, that is, opaque and not
clear, individual morals and actions will deviate from one's true nature
(ibid.). A brief summary of some characteristics of *jing* and its effect on
vital energy (*qi*) are presented in Table 4 below.

Table 4
Some Characteristics of *Jing*

Jing—various translations: inner mental attentiveness, composure, reverence, seriousness	
Characteristics:	Mental activity resonates with *li* (principle, coherence) The will controls the *qi* Pure *qi* comes into being Individuals move into a state of goodness

External cultivation

The external aspect of Learning of the Way calls for extending knowledge (*zhizhi*) and the investigation of external things and affairs (*gewu*).
This idea, taken from the *Great Learning*, calls for investigating the *li*

contained within things and affairs to the utmost (*qiongli*). Cheng Yi felt that since various *li* (coherence or pattern) were in actuality one *li*, then it is only necessary to become fully aware of the *li* of one thing or affair to enable one to perceive the coherence or pattern of all (Bol 1992).

Cheng Yi made this comment regarding the external investigation of things:

> In investigating things to exhaust their principles, the idea is not that one must exhaust completely everything in the world. If they are exhausted in only one matter, for the rest one can "*infer by analogy.*" Taking filial piety as an example, what is the reason why behavior is considered filial? If you cannot exhaust the principles in one matter, do so in another, whether you deal with an easy or a difficult example first depending on the depth of your knowledge. Just so there are innumerable paths by which you can get to the capital, and it is enough to find one of them. The reason why they can be exhausted is simply that there is one principle in all innumerable things, and even a single thing or activity, however small, has this principle. (Graham 1992, 10)

Chan translates this same passage as follows:

> To investigate things in order to understand principle to the utmost does not mean that it is necessary to investigate all things in the world. One has only to investigate the principle in one thing or event to the utmost and the principle in other things or events *can then be inferred* [emphasis added]. For example, when we talk about filial piety, we must find out what constitutes filial piety. If principle cannot be investigated to the utmost in one event, investigate another. One may begin with either the easy or the most difficult, depending on the degree of one's capacity. There are thousands of tracks and paths to the capital. Yet one can enter if he has found just one way. Principle

can be investigated to the utmost [in this way] because all
things share the same principle. Even the most insignif-
icant things and events [have] this principle. (1963, 557)

Cheng Yi felt that "To exhaust the principles of things is to study
exhaustively *why they are as they are*" (Graham 1992, 8).[46]

In describing Cheng Yi's understanding of *li* and its generalization to
external things and affairs, Graham explained Cheng Yi's understanding
as follows:

If a moral or natural principle applies to one thing we
can also apply it to other things *of the same class* [em-
phasis added] ... "extend the principle" ... or "infer by
analogy." By extending principles we learn that ultimately they are all the same, that a single principle runs
through all things. (1992, 9)

The suggestion that one could learn by *inferring from analogies* was
initially emphasized by Confucius himself. For example, the *Analects* re-
cords the following verse. Two different translations are presented below.

The ability to draw analogies from what is near at hand
can be called the way to humaneness (*Analects* 6.30).
(Keenan 2011, 101)

To know how to proceed on the analogy of what is
close at hand—this can be called the humane approach
(*Analects* 6.30). (Watson 2007, 46)

It should be noted, however, that this method of logical reasoning had been established even prior to Confucius. For example, Rošker

---

[46] A significant difference between Cheng Yi and Zhu Xi is that Cheng largely
confined his investigation of things to the mundane world, while Zhu extended the
investigation to cover the entire universe (Chan 1963, 611). See Zhu's commentary
on the *Great Learning* (Gardner 1986).

describes how "analogism" was the dominant type of Chinese logic even during the pre-Qin era (2012, 16). This period refers to the eighteen-hundred-year-plus time frame from primitive society to the establishment of the Qin Dynasty (221 BCE).

Rošker points out that analogisms maintain "the property of general analogical inference" (ibid.). Analogisms are based on the structural similarity of the item or object under investigation to the item or object referenced. The basic premise is that if two things have qualities in common, investigators can deduce or infer that the two kinds of things must likewise be identical with respect to the rest of their attributes (Rošker 2012). She further states:

> Analogical inferences are based upon the premise that reality is an organic whole composed of mutually interconnected parts which have identical or similar attributes, functions and mutually compatible structures. Analogical inferences pertain to fundamental types of deductive inferences and are an important cognitive tool that can be used to present scientific hypotheses. (ibid., 18)

By investigating and perceiving the underlying order or principles (e.g., coherence) in nature, human affairs, events, or books, one could *infer by analogy* or generalize to higher levels of abstraction. In conjunction with self-reflection, one is able to extend discovered principles to higher levels of generalization (Adler 2004).[47] A difficulty was that the typical human mind remained clouded or blocked by its physical nature.

Extending principles to the same class means to apply the reasoning in one situational context to another context under consideration. The various arts offer excellent examples of this extension of principle. In other words, similar contexts provide opportunities for applying principles, discovered previously, during the investigation of external affairs

---

[47] This method of learning, *inferring from analogies*, can be applied in practice as "studying the microscopic, understanding the macroscopic." See chapter 10 for the application of this methodology to traditional martial arts (*wushu*).

and events. For example, musical compositions and performing artists apply the extension of principles on a regular basis.

Inferring by analogy also looks for similarities, or partial similarities, in various circumstances where comparisons can be made. For instance, in various athletic events, similarities can be found from discovering and investigating principles, such as balance, patience, calmness, timing, symmetry, stages or cycles of performance, coordination and coopera-tion, and perseverance. In the cases of extending principle and inferring by analogy, principles are discovered, or examined, in one context and then extended or applied in different situational contexts.

Cheng Yi believed there were several methods that would allow one to fully realize and experience coherence, pattern, or principle:

> For everything there is a pattern; you must fully realize its pattern. There are many methods for fully realiz-ing pattern. One may read books and elucidate prin-ciples. One may discuss past and present figures and distinguish right and wrong. One may respond to affairs and things and arrange them as they should be. All are [methods of] fully realizing pattern. (Bol 1992, 321)

Chan cites this same quote in the following manner:

> There is principle in everything and one must investi-gate principle to the utmost. There are many ways to do this. One way is to read books and elucidate moral principles. Another way is to discuss people and events of the past and present, and to distinguish which are right and which are wrong. Still another way is to handle affairs and to settle them in the proper way. All these are ways to investigate the principle in things exhaustively. (1963, 561)

Cheng Yi (1033–1107), Zhu Xi's philosophical mentor, made *gewu,* or the investigation of things, a central concern in his philosophical outlook. He felt that *gewu* was the method or process that allowed individuals to obtain a comprehension of *li*, or principle (Gardner 1986). While one could, according to Cheng, "arrive at the principle in things or affairs" in a number of ways, the primary purpose or objective of "arriving at the principle in things" was moral self-development (ibid., 25). His teachings were studied and disseminated among elite intellectuals during the nearly sixty years between his death and the emergence of Zhu Xi.

Ching points out that, for Zhu, the extension of knowledge (*zhizhi*) is inseparable from the investigation of things (*gewu*). She cites the following passage by Zhu Xi:

> If we wish to extend knowledge to the utmost, we must investigate the principles of all things with which we come into contact. For the human mind and spirit is ordained to knowledge, and the things of the world all contain principles. So long as principles are not exhausted, knowledge is not yet complete. (2000, 127)

For Zhu, knowledge refers to moral knowledge, knowledge of the good, as discovered in life through the practice of reverence or inner mental attentiveness (*jing*). Table 5 summarizes some of the characteristics of the process of inferring *li* (principle or coherence) by analogy.

Table 5
Some Characteristics of Inferring *Li* by Analogy

Investigate *li* (principle, pattern, or coherence) in one thing or event. Infer by analogy to other things and events.	
Investigate *li* (principle, pattern, or coherence) in one thing or event. Apply to other things of the same class.	
This is referred to as:	Extending *li* (principle, pattern, or coherence) to different contexts Inferring by analogy Look for similarities, or partial similarities, in various circumstance in which comparisons can be made.
Inferring *li* by analogy enhances one's moral knowledge.	

Zhu Xi's mentor

Zhu Xi continued and elaborated on Cheng Yi's approach of looking for the lessons or principles found in the investigation of phenomena. Chan states that Zhu Xi's theory of the investigation of things is perhaps "the most important element in Neo-Confucian philosophy" (Chan 1987, 44). Specifically, Chan quotes this passage from Zhu Xi regarding the investigation of things:

> If we wish to extend our knowledge to the utmost, we must investigate the principles of all things we come into contact with. ... The first step ... is to instruct the learners ... in regards to all things in the world to proceed from what knowledge he has of their principles, and investigate further until he reaches the limit. After exerting himself in this way for a long time, he will one day achieve a wide and far reaching penetration.[48] (ibid.)

Eventually, two major Neo-Confucian approaches to the investigation of things emerged. These two perspectives are those of Zhu Xi and Wang Yangming. These scholars took the following approaches:

1. Zhu Xi (Chu Hsi) (1130–1200) emphasized the path of query and study. He stressed the reading of texts and the examination of the world in all its natural and social glory.
2. Wang Yangming (Wang Yang-ming) (1472–1529) suggested looking within one's self as the process for unveiling one's true human nature.

---

[48] The wide and far-reaching penetration Zhu Xi referred to is *guantong*, a comprehensive understanding of things, an integral consciousness, as described earlier. *Guantong* represents an initial or early stage of a postconventional level of consciousness (Young and Logsdon 2005).

Similarities between Zhu Xi and Wang Yangming

Both Zhu Xi and Wang Yangming *sometimes* used "*wu*" to mean affairs or events (Lee 1987). The difference between Zhu's and Wang's interpretations of *gewu* boils down to their different understanding of the linguistic unit "*ge*." Zhu took it to mean "investigate" whereas Wang interpreted it as "rectify" (ibid.). "However, it is clearly stated in the *Great Learning* that the steps of *gewu* and the extension of knowledge will eventually lead to the rectification of the heart-mind (*xin* or *hsin*). Neither Zhu nor Wang disagreed with the *Great Leaning* on this point" (ibid., 26).

Both Zhu Xi and Wang Yangming divided mind into (1) the mind of the Way, which "is manifested with the utmost subtlety and is the source of sincerity," and (2) the human mind, which has the potential for unnaturalness and insincerity (Neo-Confucian Learning and Wang Yangming 1472–1529). For example, Zhu made the distinction between the sage's mind of pure principle (the mind of the Way), and the fallible mind of the ordinary individual (de Bary 1989). Both Zhu and Wang argued for the unification of the human mind and the mind of the Way.

Both scholars, and their respective schools, also shared the assumption that there was a direct link between personal cultivation and an understanding of natural and moral order (Hall and Ames 1998). Specifically, both schools proposed that the more thorough one's personal cultivation, the greater one's understanding of natural and moral order. Both schools edited and rewrote different aspects of Confucian volumes and texts, tried to clarify concepts and ideas of Confucianism, and helped to develop spiritual dimensions of Confucians (*jingzuo*).[49]

Next, the teachings of Zhu Xi and Wang Yangming are examined in greater detail.

---

[49] For more on *jingzuo*, see http://en.wikipedia.org/wiki/Jing_zuo, 2009.

CHAPTER 5

The Approaches of Zhu Xi and Wang Yangming

The different approaches of Zhu Xi and Wang Yangming regarding how to examine principle (*li*) have been the subject of inquiry for centuries. Their different methods are briefly examined here to provide the reader with a more complete understanding of these two historically important perspectives.

Zhu Xi (Chu Hsi) (1130–1200)

The Neo-Confucianism of Zhu Xi has impacted China significantly for seven hundred years (Chan 1987).[50] He gave Confucianism new meaning, which in turn influenced not only Chinese thought but also made a considerable impression on thought in Korea and Japan (Chan 1963). His philosophical outlook merged the philosophies of five earlier Northern Song Dynasty (960–1127)[51] scholars: Zhou Dunyi (Chou Tuni) (1017–1073), Cheng Hao (Ch'eng Hao) (1032–1085), Cheng Yi (Ch'eng I) (1033–1107), Zhang Zai (Chang Tsai) (1020–1077), and Shao Yong (Shao Yung) (1011–1077) (Chan 1987). One of his most important innovations was the designation of the *Great Learning*, the *Analects*, the *Mencius*,

---

[50] De Bary (1975) suggests that "the most important manual of Neo-Confucian teaching" is Zhu Xi's *Reflections on Things at Hand* (153).

[51] The Song Dynasty ruled China from 960 to 1279. The Northern Song ruled from 960 to 1127. After the Song lost control of the north, the Southern Song ruled from 1127 to 1279.

and the *Doctrine of the Mean* as the Four Books in 1190. Since that time, Confucian thought and discussions have centered on these four texts.[52], [53]

Zhu Xi represented the systematic and theoretical wing of Neo-Confucianism, referred to as the Cheng-Zhu School. In fact, his contribution to the Neo-Confucian school was his development of a methodical process of self-cultivation (Gardner 1986). This program, or method, of self-cultivation evolved principally from his study of the *Great Learning*.

Zhu felt that the goal of self-cultivation was to keep one's inborn luminous virtue, which is in every human being, unobscured. He felt that progress along the Confucian Way (*Dao*) requires a state of psychic equilibrium, a state in which the heart-mind (*xin* or *hsin*) reflects original human goodness and enables the seeker to pursue and acquire sagehood (Ching 2000). Ching (2000) felt that Zhu's teaching on equilibrium and harmony was at the heart of his philosophy. This is why the attainment of psychic equilibrium plays such an important role in Neo-Confucian self-cultivation. Zhu believed that such equilibrium can be achieved if individuals attain either *weifa* or *yifa* states of consciousness.

Weifa and *yifa* consciousness

The *weifa* state of consciousness is discussed in the *Doctrine of the Mean*, one of Zhu's favorite texts. Confucians actively participate in their own personal transformations as they strive to achieve either *weifa* or *yifa* states of consciousness. *Weifa* is a deeper state than *yifa*. *Weifa* is a state of pure consciousness that reflects original human goodness before the rise of emotions. "It is an experience that goes beyond being conscious

---

[52] The Chinese civil service exam system began under the reign of Emperor Wu (140–87 BCE). These exams were based on Confucian texts. However, from 1313 to 1905, the imperial civil service exams were based on the Four Books. The Four Books were also important in the development of formal school education. Zhu's philosophy survived the Intellectual Revolution of 1917 and even became the foundation of Professor Feng Youlan's new rationalism of the 1930s (Chan 1963).

[53] Zhu Xi suggested that Confucian students should read these texts in the following order: the *Great Learning*, the *Analects*, the *Mencius*, and the *Doctrine of the Mean*. However, the first national civil service examination system, based on the Confucian canon in general, was established in 606 (Keenan 2011).

of what is occurring, to simply being conscious" (Ching 2000, 116). It is a status of consciousness that is "free of emotions, concepts, and images" (ibid., 261). *Weifa* is a state of consciousness of ultimate reality; it represents a mystical experience.[54]

Kim describes *weifa* consciousness as being in the preintentional realm. He suggests that Zhu Xi believed that *weifa* consciousness was "preintentional" because it exits before selfish desires for outside goods and other selfish tendencies emerge. Kim states that, according to Zhu:

> All human beings possess this mind which in its *weifa*
> state is the repository of all principles, regardless of one's
> character or psycho-physical disposition. The *weifa* state
> of the mind is a given condition for all humans without
> fail, from sages to ordinary people. (2013, 125–126)

Zhu Xi felt that it was only through study and moral effort (*gongfu*) that individuals were able to transmute turbid *qi* into clear *qi* and hence reveal their *weifa* states of consciousness. This text prefers Ching's description of the *weifa* state cited above as a state that is "free of emotions, concepts, and images" (Ching 2000, 116).

Yifa, on the other hand, can be experienced after the rise of emotions. It represents a state of emotions in harmony. While *weifa* is a state that is difficult to attain and is somewhat more hypothetical, *yifa* is a state of emotional harmony that can be actualized (ibid, 261–262).

Zhu's interpretation of *weifa* and *yifa* was that the two states represent the same reality, and both states reflect the status of the mind (Ching 2000). Zhu's doctrine centered on the practice of inner mental attentiveness (*jing*)[55] and study. From 1170 until his death in 1200, he focused more on Cheng Yi's exhortation to abide in inner mental attentiveness

---

[54] *Weifa* seems to be a *state* of consciousness or a "peak experience" (James 1941). Peak experiences can occur, for example, when witnessing a sunset or sunrise; observing a fine-arts performance; or practicing *wushu*, during meditation, or quiet sitting. These somewhat temporary states of consciousness are different from *quantong,* which represents a more permanently acquired *level* of consciousness, or worldview. Attaining a state of *weifa* consciousness on a permanent basis is rare.

[55] Also translated as composure, reverence, and seriousness.

as well as external knowledge. This approach provided more of a balance between contemplation and action. From this perspective, meditation or quiet sitting was seen as a means for achieving inner mental attentiveness. Inner mental attentiveness (*jing*) was to be applied to an active life.

Further, he felt that those individuals who are able to preserve their inborn luminous virtue will subsequently extend their grace to others and thereby enable the populace to preserve their inborn luminous virtue (Gardner 1986). Each individual strived to maintain or regain contact with his or her original good mind and nature (ibid.).

Gewu (ko-wu) means the investigation of things

In his doctrine of the investigation of things, Zhu carefully followed his mentor Cheng Yi (Chan 1963).[56] Zhu was quite influential in this Rational School of thought, and when referring to the investigation of things, he emphasized book learning. Lee (1987) explains that for Zhu, after the successful investigation of things, one knows right from wrong, and is thus morally awakened . While Zhu emphasized the reading of texts, it was also true that "virtually anything, from current events and the affairs of daily life to the sayings and writings of the ancient sages, could be matter for the investigation of principle" (Kalton 2004, 192).[57]

Zhu Xi described the impartiality and comprehensive knowledge that can be attained through *gewu* by using the analogy of a candle. He explained this impartiality and comprehensive knowledge as follows:

> It is like lighting a wax candle in the middle [of the room]. The light penetrates so that no spot is left unilluminated. Although one wishes to bring a bad thing in, there is no place to put it [where it cannot be detected]. Naturally there is no place for it. When knowledge is not completed it is like putting a shade on the lamp. Then

---

[56] He also followed Cheng Yi's position regarding the doctrine of principle (Chan 1963, 591).

[57] Munro states, "For Zhu, the objects of knowledge or study can be concrete things (a bamboo plant), a relationship (father-son) or an idea in a text" (2005, 23).

you can see as far as the light reaches. Where the light
does not reach, everything is dark, and you cannot see.
Although there is a thing or affair beyond it, you cannot
know it. (Munro 2005, 23–24)

Zhu advocated the investigation of things through the process of
"disinterested study" of Confucian values and texts. Disinterested study
is in contrast to "vocational study," which is intended to further one's
career (Gardner 1990).[58] Zhu took the word *zhi* (extension) to mean expansion or increase. He considered the expansion of knowledge (*zhizhi*)
to be the extension of knowledge (Lee 1987). He was thorough in stress-
ing both *deductive* and *inductive* methods for the investigation of things
(Chan 1967). For instance, the investigation of things utilizes a deductive
approach in the sense that practitioners can begin with preconceived
principles (*li*), such as harmony, balance, equilibrium, *yin-yang* theory,
spontaneity, unity, wholeness, and change, and they can then search for
observations or applications of the concepts. Similarly, practitioners can
investigate things, activities, and events utilizing an inductive approach,
and in the process, they can discover principles (*li*) from their empirical
observations. In reality both approaches can be intermingled because
the deductive investigation of things entails elements of the inductive
method, and vice versa.

Zhu Xi also equally emphasized *objective* observation and *intuitive*
understanding (Chan 1963). In the case of objective understanding, he
observed phenomena that in turn led to the discovery and examination
of principles or coherence (*li*). In the case of intuitive understanding, he
recognized that individuals could also acquire an understanding and
appreciation of *li* without using reasoning.[59] Table 6 presents the methods
of inquiry and ways of understanding recognized by Zhu Xi.

---

[58] "Disinterested study" will be explored in greater detail in chapter 8, "The Process
of *Kungfu*."

[59] *Intuition* can be defined as a direct perception of truth or fact, in this case *li*,
independent of any reasoning process. It represents an immediate apprehension
or understanding.

Table 6
Approaches to the Investigation of Things Recognized by Zhu Xi

Ways of Understanding

	Objective	Intuitive
Deductive		
Inductive		

Methods of Inquiry

Examples of *li* (principles or coherence) that can be examined deductively or inductively, and apprehended objectively or intuitively, include harmony, balance, equilibrium, *yin-yang* theory, spontaneity, unity, wholeness, and change.

For Zhu, "To investigate things is to discover exhaustively that this event ought to be done in this way and that event ought to be done in that way ..." (Lee 1987, 26). He stated that *zhizhi* "is to extend our knowledge to the utmost with the desire that it become(s) completely exhaustive" (Gardner 1986, 92). He interpreted *li* (principle or coherence) to be abstract entities in things (and events). These principles or coherence are the objects of the investigation of things. The prudent thing to do, according to Zhu, is to inquire exhaustively into an affair, event, or activity (i.e., to investigate things thoroughly).

According to Zhu Xi's metaphysics, "there is no *wu* (thing) in this world that does not have *li* (principles or coherence) and each *shih* (event) also has its own principles" (Lee 1987, 27). To investigate things is to investigate systematically and exhaustively the principles inherent in things, events, or activities. Once the principles inherent in a thing or event are grasped, according to Zhu, we will somehow know right and wrong with regard to *that* thing or event (ibid.). Lee translates Zhu as follows:

> Although each event has a way that it should be which is unalterable, still we ought to seek the reason why it should be so. The reason why it should be so is *li* (principle). The *li* is such, therefore, that it [the way the event should be] cannot be changed. (ibid.)

Zhu Xi maintained that the investigation of things is a means for us to expand our knowledge, moral or otherwise. He said, "The reason for investigating things (*gewu*) is to extend knowledge (*zhizhi*) ... The more principles that I discover, the more extensive my knowledge will be" (ibid.). He suggests that during the process of investigating things, affairs, and events, principles in the individual's heart-mind (*xin* or *hsin*) are brought into resonance with, and made coherent with, principles (*li*) within the things, affairs, and events themselves. Over time this practice leads the individual on a path of moral development.

Zhu felt that *gewu* (the investigation of things) was the means to *zhizhi* (extended knowledge). He stated, "If we wish to extend our knowledge to the utmost, we must probe thoroughly the principle in things we encounter" (Gardner 1986, 54). He interpreted the *Great Learning* to suggest that *gewu* was the first action in the self-cultivation process, leading toward a moral awakening (Gardner 1986).

Moral awakening

The primary objective of Zhu's "learning of the heart/mind" was to ensure that the "human mind," which is endowed in the "psychophysically discrete individual, becomes more closely aligned with the mind of *Tao* (*Dao*)" which reflects the unity or wholeness of principle (*li*) (Bloom 1985, 310). His primary concern was how one can learn to be a sage, that is, how one can learn to be fully moral (Gardner 1990). Apprehending the principle in things of the world—books, nature, history, human relationships, and so forth—was the first and most critical step in self-refinement (ibid.). He felt that *gewu* (the investigation of things) is the gate between dreaming and awakening. When things are investigated, then, one becomes awakened; otherwise, one is in a dream (Lee 1987). Like Buddhist meditation, the investigation of things (*gewu*) leads to self-realization, an enlightened state. However, unlike Buddhist meditation, *gewu* is a reality-affirming process, a process that underscores the relationship between the individual self and others (Gardner 1986).[60]

Therefore, Zhu felt that when *gewu* was practiced properly, it too would ultimately lead to an enlightened state. Gardner (1986, 56) quotes Zhu Xi in describing this state:

> The manifest and the hidden, the subtle and obvious qualities of all things will be known, and the mind, in its whole substance and vast operations, will be completely illuminated.

Achieving this state, according to Zhu, required equally mental composure (*jing*) and the exhaustive study of external principles (*gewu*) (Gardner 1986).

Seeking principles

The Cheng-Zhu School favored broad text-based learning and the investigation of things (Hall and Ames 1998). Zhu Xi did not rule out introspection as a means to illumination; however, his emphasis was on scholarly learning, and this learning encompasses the investigation of the principles

---

[60] According to Zhu's understanding, individuals had to immerse themselves in the examination of the external world. He felt that his approach was in contrast to the Buddhist approach of introspection (Gardner 1986).

(coherence) of all things with which we come into contact. This means that in all affairs and things, the individual should seek fundamental principles and use his or her mind in the quest of principles in things and affairs.

Zhu felt that sincerity of mind could be achieved through the investigation of things, the extensive reading of Confucian texts, and the gradual grasping of the spontaneous practice of Heavenly principles (*tianli*). While he believed in the diversity of principles (coherence) in events and things, ultimately, like his mentor Cheng Yi, he felt that all principles would boil down to the same.

According to Zhu, in order to achieve enlightenment, an individual must actively seek knowledge, investigate ideas/events, meditate on them, and then investigate some more (*Jingzuo*, Wikipedia 2009). In keeping with this understanding, spiritual and moral development is like a cyclical journey of tranquility and activity, or of preserving the mind and investigating principles, or of knowledge and action (Yao 2000).[61]

In summary, according to Bol (2008), Zhu made three assertions that identify *li* (principle or coherence) as fundamental to learning:

1. Every thing and event has its own *li*. In other words, every thing and event has its own principle, logic, norm, or standard; every thing and event has its own coherence.
2. It is possible for the mind to see and comprehend the *li*, or coherence, of things and events with certainty.
3. Ultimately, all *li* are one li.[62]

The following quote from Zhu Xi helps to explain why he believed that the unity of *li* was so important:

> [Let us consider the idea that one] extends one's knowledge by apprehending the coherence of things (*gewu*).

---

[61] Chapter 1 describes in greater detail the cyclical nature of "Confucian Self-Cultivation."

[62] The Cheng brothers (Cheng Yi, 1033–1107, and Cheng Hao, 1032–1085) also made these three assertions. They are the scholars who inspired Zhu Xi and for whom the Cheng-Zhu School of Neo-Confucianism is named.

> [One possibility is this means] that with respect to one thing, one exhaustively attains one portion of coherence, and thus one's knowledge gains one portion; with respect to a second thing, one exhaustively [attains] a second portion of coherence, and thus one's knowledge gains a second portion; the more things' coherences one can exhaustively attain, the broader one's knowledge will be. [However, this is not the case.] In fact, there is just one coherence, and "when you understand 'this,' 'that' is also clear." Therefore, the *Great Learning* said, "The extension of knowledge lies in apprehending the coherence of things," and did not say "If you want to extend your knowledge in a particular respect, the way lies in apprehending the coherence of a particular thing." (Zhu 1997, as cited in Angle 2009, 45)

In other words, as we can see from Zhu's perspective, Neo-Confucianism relies on broad self-cultivation outcomes that stem from focused inquiry and attention. Zhu developed this concept from the focus on external things and affairs. It was his belief that this focused inquiry and attention, if approached properly, leads to moral, social, and spiritual development.

His critics, however, argued that his theory of the examination of things externalized the study of principle (*li*). They contended that self-cultivation, leading toward greater self-knowledge, must begin with the "rectification" of the heart-mind before it becomes hopelessly lost in the minutia of the mundane world. Wang Yangming was a major proponent of this alternative perspective. In contrast to Zhu Xi, Wang Yangming maintained that the extension of knowledge is not a matter of generating knowledge—moral or otherwise.

Wang Yangming (Wang Yang-ming) (1472–1529)

The Lu[63]-Wang School of Neo-Confucianism rejected the study of official or canonical texts for a more subjective, meditative approach to personal realization (Hall and Ames 1998). Wang Yangming was very influential in this Idealistic School of thought, and it was his conviction that it was futile to investigate external objects and events in order to gain moral insights (Lee 1987, 32).

He ignored the nuanced differences between things in the world and instead recommended a holistic, intuitive understanding without external knowledge. When developed to its extreme, Wang Yangming's thought resembled Chan Buddhism, with its emphasis on meditation, sudden awakening, and the elimination of intellectual concepts and divisions between the self and the outside world.

Wang suggested that the real task of the scholar was to cultivate the heart-mind (*xin* or *hsin*). In other words, he felt that rather than looking for the principle of things in the outside world, practitioners needed to search their heart-minds. His premise was that we can only find principle in our heart-minds, and when we scrutinize our heart-minds, we find them filled with emotions (Berthong and Berthong 2000). Hence, he placed his emphasis on internal cultivation, believing that the human mind is both the locus and the standard of sagehood.

Wang's most celebrated theme was his firm belief in the continuity and inseparability of knowledge and action (Hall and Ames 1998). He had more confidence in our *liangzhi* (innate knowledge of good or innate moral intuition) and felt that, in its original state, it can provide us with all moral knowledge without having to acquire knowledge from external

---

[63] Lu refers to Lu Jiuyan (Lu Chiu-yüan) (1139–1192), considered one of the founders of the Lu-Wang School of the Mind. Both Lu Jiuyan, Zhu Xi's contemporary, and Wang Yangming, of the Ming Dynasty, pointed out the difficulty inherent in any doctrine that gives too much emphasis to intellectual striving; for example, *gewu*. In their opinion, such doctrines made intellectuals of all sages. They felt that this approach made it difficult for individuals who were deprived of opportunities to study and that it put them at a disadvantage in their quest for sagehood (Ching 1986, 76). Lu and Wang went so far as to suggest that book learning was almost a distraction from the quest for sagehood.

sources.[64] This knowledge, he felt, was intrinsic in the human mind and cannot be obtained by learning (Lee 1987). Such innate knowledge (*liangzhi*) is possessed *in toto* from infancy. However, it is obscured (Lee 1989). "Fundamentally, *liangzhi* is a native ability to distinguish right from wrong, as well as good from bad" (Cua 2003b, 770).

Principles exist in the heart-mind

Wang denies that principles (*li*) exist in things other than the heart-mind. Therefore, to look for principles (*li*) in things is to divide the mind and principle into two. His supposition that principles reside in the heart-mind obliged him to contest that principles (*li*) exist in external things (Lee 1987). Once the obscurities of our innate knowledge (*liangzhi*) have been cleared, that knowledge is reclaimed rather than acquired (ibid.). Our *liangzhi*, when it is not clouded by selfish desires, is like a bright mirror and can tell us right from wrong when it responds to a particular situation (ibid.).

Gewu (ko-wu) means to "rectify things"

This is how Wang interpreted *gewu*. For him, one had to already know right from wrong before one could perform *gewu*. He also felt that *zhizhi* (extension of knowledge) was not a matter of increasing our knowledge but, rather, of clearing our innate moral knowledge (*liangzhi*). When we respond to a particular situation, regardless of its nature, with clear *liangzhi*, it will tell us which action or decision is the right approach, without first having to stockpile moral knowledge. An individual should only worry about his or her mind not being clear and not about an inability to respond to all changing conditions.

For Wang, the effort of clearing one's mind is called *zhizhi*. Our road to sagehood, therefore, requires that we first clear up whatever clouds our *liangzhi* (innate knowledge). The premise of Wang's *zhizhi* (clearing the

---

[64] Julia Ching (1976) interpreted the *liangzhi* of Wang Yangming this way: "[I]t is that in man which enables him to discern between right and wrong, an inborn capacity to know and do the good, a capacity to be developed as well as a goal to be attained, since the perfect development of *liang-chi* [*liangzhi*] signifies sagehood" (267).

mind) and *gewu* (rectifying things) is that we should act according to what our *liangzhi* tells us to do (Lee 1987). The effort put forth in both (a) clearing one's mind and (b) rectifying things is intended to overcome selfish ideas.

Follow the guidance of our innate knowledge

Wang says that to follow the guidance of our *liangzhi* (innate knowledge) is to both *zhizhi* (clear one's mind) and *gewu* (rectify things or make things right) (Lee, 1987.). To extend knowledge is to transform *liangzhi* into action.[65] For example, to know the proper way to care for one's parents is knowledge. However, this knowledge must be put into practice and transformed into action before one can say that he or she has extended knowledge (ibid.). The effort of *zhizhi* and *gewu* is simultaneously an effort to put good knowledge into practice as well as to control the selfish desires that could cloud one's *liangzhi* (ibid.). The realization of *Dao* depends on one's effort and the extension of one's *liangzhi* (Cua 2003b).

Wang interprets *wu* to mean an event. If a person's *liangzhi* tells him or her that the right action is A, the realization of the act of doing A is that individual's *gewu* (rectification of things or events). On the other hand, if something should be done but is not done, things are not rectified or made right.

Lee (1987) suggests that for Wang, one must first be morally awake before one can undertake any acts to transform his or her knowledge into action. Therefore, for him, the extension of knowledge necessarily consists of action. His concept of *li* was that it was inside every person, and reflection on *li* is the only way to enlightenment. He felt that it was correct to search for sagehood within one's self, and there was no need to seek sagehood in things and affairs outside. Principles of things (*li*) are not to be found external to the mind.

The following quotes, by Wang Yangming, from the *East Asian History Sourcebook* (2009) help to clarify his philosophy:

---

[65] Wang experienced his own sudden enlightenment, or instantaneous insight, into the meaning of "the investigation of things" (*gewu*), at the age of thirty-seven. He began teaching the unity of knowledge and action one year later, at age thirty-eight (Cua 2003b).

> What I say about extending knowledge to the utmost through the investigation of things means extending and developing my intuitive knowledge of good to the utmost on all affairs and things.
>
> In the unity and mutual development of knowledge and practice, no distinction can be made. The principles of things and affairs are not to be found external to the mind.

Wang believed that sincerity of mind could be achieved "more naturally" without the extensive reading of books. He proposed the cultivation of one's intuition, "extending one's innate knowing to the utmost" (de Bary 1991, 846). Wang Ken (*ca.* 1483–1540), a follower of Wang Yangming, argued for the necessity of scholarly associations and independent schools so the Way could be discussed and studied (de Bary 1991).

De Bary (1989) comments on some summary differences between Wang Yangming and Zhu Xi as follows.

Wang:
1. Insisted on the unity, stability, and quiescence of the mind, and
2. Felt that the mind and principle were not only inseparable but also were identical.

On the other hand, Zhu:
1. Emphasized the fallibility of the human mind and the subtlety of the Mind of the Way, and
2. Saw the need for the objective investigation of things and affairs.

Pursuing the inclination of Zhu Xi, during the Qing Dynasty (1644–1911), Chinese society began the investigation of things using numerous avenues and approaches. Individuals utilized various vehicles or methodologies for investigating things external to the mind. When investigating external things, affairs, and events, Neo-Confucians searched for, discovered, and examined the concept of *li* (coherence, principles, or patterns).

CHAPTER 6

Neo-Confucian *Li*

Discovering and examining *li* (coherence, principles, or patterns) was a major component of what became the orthodox approach of the Cheng-Zhu School of Neo-Confucianism. This process of discovering and examining *li* is described in greater detail in this chapter.

Li—Principle or Coherence

Exploring *li*

The concept of *li* represents a major idea in the process of investigating things. Zhu Xi and Wang Yangming examined this Neo-Confucian concept (*gewu*) and reached different conclusions. Earlier in this text, Angle's definition of Neo-Confucian *li* was cited as "the valuable, intelligible way that things fit together" (2009, 32). Angle's definition is more in line with the Cheng-Zhu School, which became the orthodox interpretation of *li*. From this perspective, *li* is present in "things" and in processes. For example, Angle (2009, 124) suggests that "*li* is about patterns through time and space ..." *Li* is a *descriptive* term that refers to how something works (Bol 2008). It represents the logic, reasoning, or coherence of a statement, the actual pattern or system of relationships that holds parts together (ibid.).

Likewise *li* is used as a *normative* expression. In this sense, *li* can refer to a standard according to which something should function and thereby ensure that all parts work together. Both of the Cheng brothers stressed the idea that *li* is changeless, that behind the continual flux of the visible universe there are "constant principles," "fixed principles," "real principles" (Graham 1992, 14). In summary, *li* is an expression that is (a) descriptive because it describes how things actually work, and (b) normative because it explains how things should work (Bol 2008).

Graham cites the scholar Xu Heng (Hsü Hêng) (1209–1281) who explained how the concept of *li* could in fact represent both normative and descriptive ideas. Hsü Hêng stated:

> That by which something is as it is [descriptive] and that to which it should conform [normative] is the explanation of the word *li*. That by which it is as it is, is the source—the decree; that to which it should conform is the outflow— morality. Every single activity and thing must have a [principle] by which it is as it is, and to which it should conform. (1992, 29–30)

Wang Tingxiang (Wang T'ing-hsiang) (1474–1544), an intellectual of the Ming Dynasty (1368–1644), asserted that each thing and event had its own principle (Zhang 2002). In other words, different things have different principles (ibid.).[66] Finally, Dai Zhen (Tai Chen) (1724–1777), a notable scholar during the Qing (Ching) Dynasty (1644–1912), believed that principle (*li*) represented the differences between things. He felt that the principles of things should be derived by the examination of things to the smallest detail (Zhang 2002, 41).[67]

Learning and *li*

Returning once again to the concept and practice of Neo-Confucian learning, we see that there is a fundamental tension between the internal and external aspects of learning. On the one hand, internal learning can be seen as attempting to attain and maintain an internal state of

---

[66] This idea did not suit the traditional intellectuals of his era.

[67] Dai Zhen was considered by many to be the most important scholar of the Qing Dynasty. He was a prominent critic of Confucian orthodoxy of the Song and Ming dynasties.

coherence (equilibrium) in which one's heart-mind (*xin* or *hsin*) achieves and preserves its own original nature. In this view, suggested by Wang Yangming and others, learning begins by examining one's own heart-mind[68] (Bol 2008).

On the other hand, Zhu Xi suggested that learning amounts to the cumulative effort one asserts, over time, investigating external things. This external investigation of things represents a process that gradually expands one's heart-mind. This expanded awareness enables one to eventually see the *li* (principle or coherence) in all external things, affairs, and events—and ultimately the coherence in one's own mind (Bol 2008).

Zhu believed that the external investigation of things represents a process by which principles (*li*) of the mind are brought into contact, and into coherence with, principles in things, affairs, and events. Through this process of investigation, one could develop one's learning capacity and understanding to its fullest extent (de Bary 1989).[69]

This exhaustive learning of principle (*li*) suggests that "one may use what one already knows" to reach a comprehensive understanding of things (Cheng 2003, 624). In order to achieve this comprehensive understanding, learners "must see that all things are related through principles [*li*] and that all principles are related" (ibid.). Using this methodology, one will discover that recognizing and comprehending a single principle (*li*) can lead to the discovery of other principles (ibid.).

Further, Zhu felt that an open mind and quiet reflection were essential in order to effectively probe *li* (Gardner 1990). Both Zhu's and Wang's approaches implied a gradual learning (development) process that took place over time (Angle 2009).

Successful Neo-Confucian learning developed an ability to intuit harmonious relationships between parts and affairs, operating successfully within the context of a larger, self-sustaining, organic whole (Bol

---

[68] Recall that earlier the heart-mind (*xin* or *hsin*) was described as being broader than the problem-solving mind (*yi*). The heart-mind not only encompasses one's problem-solving abilities but also includes the totality of one's emotions.

[69] When principles (*li*) are examined exhaustively, in order to understand their order, this process is referred to as *qiongli* (*ch'iung-li*). The purpose of *qiongli* is to "fulfill the functions and potential of the mind ..." (Cheng 2003, 623).

2008).[70] The Cheng-Zhu School believed that the way, or manner, in which the coherence of any thing or event systematically "fits" or inter-relates with the coherence of any other thing or event can be discovered (Angle 2009). Hence, comprehending *li* is about understanding patterns through time and space (ibid.).

The Cheng-Zhu School also believed, as a worldview, that every thing and affair had its norm. They felt that all things are comprised of vital energy (*qi* or *chi*); however, *li* (principle or coherence) determine how things and events operate and how they should function (Bol 2008). However, as de Bary (1989) points out, unfortunately individuals and entities who pursue utilitarian advantages and shallow, shortsighted self-interests rarely have any notion of the concept of principle or coherence (*li*). Such individuals and entities frequently treat other humans as animals in their decision-making and problem-solving. Table 7 presents a summary of some additional characteristics of Neo-Confucian *li*.

Table 7
Some Additional Characteristics of *Li*

Li is descriptive.	Refers to how parts actually work Describes system of relationships that hold parts together
Li is normative.	Refers to how parts should work together
Through the investigation of things: *Li* (coherence, principles) of the mind ~*Li* (coherence, principles) in things, affairs, events.	

~ means "is congruent with"

---

[70] Roger T. Ames and David L. Hall discuss how an interactive field of processes and events can be understood by utilizing a "focus and field" perspective. They describe how this perspective is pervasive in both Confucian and Taoist philosophy (2001; 2003).

The Unity of *Li*

The *li* of Heaven (*tianli*)

Neo-Confucians believed that the *li* of every thing and affair is part of the *li* of the universe, *tianli*, which translates as the *li* of Heaven[71] (Bol 2008). Further, the universe is an integrated system in which all principles (*li*) are united. Neo-Confucians felt that when an individual's mind was exercised to its fullest, without error, one's mind would experience *tianli*, the Principle of Heaven, which penetrates all things and affairs (Chen 1986). For example, Cheng Hao, one of Zhu Xi's intellectual mentors, believed that humanity formed "one body with heaven and earth and all things" (de Bary 1975, 151). Both Cheng and Zhu believed that this principle penetrated all things and affairs. Conceptually, they felt that *li* is distinct from and prior to *qi* (*chi*), or vital energy. In other words, the *li* for everything is inherent in the universe before things come into being (Bol 2008). Zhu quoted Cheng Hao as saying, "Although I have learned certain things from teachers, I have discovered myself the meaning of the two words *Tien-li* [*tianli*] through personal reflection and experience" (Ching 2000).[72] Zhu Xi felt that, at birth, humans are endowed with Heavenly principle, and that human passions emerge later. This immanent heavenly principle remains latent in most people and, in his opinion, is made manifest by self-cultivation (ibid., 98).

Zhu felt that Heavenly principle was the principle of the highest good and was another name for the Great Ultimate (*taiji*). He is quoted as saying, "The Great Ultimate is only the principle of Heaven and earth and all things. There is a Great Ultimate in Heaven and earth and there is a Great Ultimate in each of the myriad things" (Ching 2000, 60).

Zhu Zi viewed *taiji* (the Great Ultimate) as the Supreme Polarity. This Supreme Polarity—the principle of *yin/yang*—is ultimately a "single 'nondualistic' principle of coherence," the "fundamental ordering

---

[71] Earlier it was noted that *tianli* also can be translated as "Heavenly principle, ultimate principle, or norm of the good or perfect" (Tu and Tucker 2004, 511).

[72] It should be noted that the term "Heaven" (*tian*) represented the cosmos, which includes the earth. The term did not refer to an afterlife as is the case in Christianity.

principle which is inherent in all things, including the human mind" (Adler 2004, 129).

Chan quotes Zhu with respect to the Great Ultimate:

> The Great Ultimate is merely the principle of heaven and earth and the myriad things. With respect to heaven and earth, there is the Great Ultimate in them. With respect to the myriad things, there is the Great Ultimate in each and every one of them. Before heaven and earth existed, there was assuredly this principle. It is the principle that "through movement generates the yang." It is also this principle that "through tranquility generates the yin." (1963, 638)

Professor Wm. Theodore de Bary (2004, 94) cites Professor Wing-tsit Chan's translation of Zhu Xi's view of the Supreme Ultimate (i.e., the Great Ultimate or *taiji*) as follows:

> According to [Zhu Xi], the Supreme Ultimate [Great Ultimate or *taiji*] is at once the one principle and the sum total of all principles. At the same time, since everything has principle, everything has the Supreme Ultimate in it. Consequently, the Supreme Ultimate involves all things as a whole and at the same time every individual thing involves the Supreme Ultimate. In other words, the universe is a macrocosm while everything is a microcosm. In a sense the pattern was hinted [at] by Zhou Dunyi in his *Tongshu* [Comprehending the Changes] where he said, "The many are [ultimately] one and the one is actually differentiated in the many. The one and the many each has its own correct state of being. The great and the small each has its definite function.

The above two citations summarize Zhu Xi's perspective on the concept of wholeness.

Specifically, Zhu Xi felt that *li* is both immanent (is within) and transcendent to *qi* (Chan 1987). He felt that in the universe, there has never been *qi* (vital energy) without *li* (principle) or *li* without *qi* (Chan 1987). Bol (2008) suggests that the Neo-Confucian concept of *li* resembled what contemporary scientists refer to as a "unified field theory" or a "theory of everything."

Seeking *tianli*

In seeking *li*, Zhu Xi was looking for a more abstract and a more universal truth—a principle of Heaven. Zhu was searching for a universal truth that was both immanent and transcendent in the cosmos. He was investigating Neo-Confucian *li*, the principle or coherence, that lay beneath and gave unity to the world (Gardner 1986). Zhu was seeking to discover and experience the *tianli* (principle of Heaven) that underlays all things in the universe. His was a search for a truth that was inherent in all things and affairs in the cosmos (Gardner 1990).

Zhu is cited as saying, "The cultivation of the essential and the examination of the difference between the Principle of Nature (*Tianli*, Principle of Heaven) and human selfish desires are things that must not be interrupted for a single movement in the course of our daily activities and movement and rest" (Chan 1963, 605). Confucians felt that in order to become humane, they had to "preserve" and "nurture" the Principle of Heaven (*tianli*) within their own heart-minds (*xin*) (Ching 1986b).

Similarly, Cheng Yi (1033–1107), cofounder of the Cheng-Zhu School[73] of Neo-Confucian thought, held to the fundamental belief that moral truth was immanent in all things and affairs. He also felt there was one absolute and ultimately knowable *li* (principle). It was Cheng Yi who suggested that "principle is one, its manifestations many" (Gardner 1990, 73). In terms of extending one's learning, we see that "if a moral or natural principle applies to one thing we can also apply it to other things of the same class ... 'extend the principle' or '*infer by analogy.*' By extending discovered principles, we learn that ultimately they are all the same, "that a single principle runs through all things" (Graham 1992,

---

[73] The Cheng-Zhu School of Neo-Confucian thought is named after the Cheng brothers (Cheng Yi, 1033–1107, and Cheng Hao, 1032–1085) and Zhu Xi (1130–1200).

9). Cheng Yi's statement regarding the unity of *li* was adapted from a prior Buddhist use of the term (Angle 2009). He asserted the ultimate oneness of moral principle and suggested comprehending the moral principle of the universe by investigating principles in all things. Zhu Xi found Cheng Yi's approach to be compelling and subsequently made it the basis of his own perspective (Gardner 1990). While both Zhu Xi (1130–1200) and Wang Yangming (1472–1529) believed in the concept of the unity of *li* (principle), they disagreed on how to examine and cultivate the universal *li*.

Finally, all of the great Confucian teachers agreed that the honoring of nature and the path of inquiry and study could not be separated. Some individuals simply needed more reflection on the will, or internal consciousness, while others needed the discipline of textual and external study (Berthong and Berthong 2000). Attempting to fulfill the unity of mind and principle (*li*) was a lifelong project. After all, it took Confucius fifty-five years, from age fifteen until seventy, before he reached the stage of effortless and easy nontransgression (de Bary 1989).

Neo-Confucian practitioners felt there were several approaches, or paths, that individuals could embark upon for investigating things and discovering principles (*li*). Some of these potential paths are examined next.

CHAPTER 7

Selecting a Vehicle or Path
for Self-Cultivation

There are many forms or methods of self-cultivation (Berthong and Berthong 2000), primarily because "people are unique" (Tu 1985, 61). Just as there are no identical faces, there are as many means of self-cultivation as there are human beings (Tu 1985). Confucians employ a variety of practices for maintaining watchfulness over their heart- minds. Hence, it is impossible to establish a fixed model by which all people can learn to experience the Way (Tu 1989). However, "steadfastness of purpose" is the most important attribute for self-cultivation. Neo-Confucian practices for self-improvement are anchored in philosophical theory and are intended to change the practitioner's worldview (Angle 2009).

The Arts as Vehicles for Self-Cultivation

Evolution of the arts

Confucian learning is both active and reflective and as such can be engaged in while learning and performing the arts. Historically, the six arts represented activities to be performed, as well as subjects to be mastered. According to de Bary and Bloom (1999) and Chan (1963), it is generally accepted that "the six arts" were traditionally considered: ritual or ceremony, music, archery, charioteering or carriage-driving, calligraphy or writing, and arithmetic or mathematics. The scholar Liu Yin (1249–1293) observed that the meaning of the "arts" had undergone a fundamental change since the time of Confucius. He pointed out that while Confucius originally used the term to refer to practices of ritual, music, archery, charioting, and painting, during Liu Yin's time (1249–1293), the term primarily included poetry, prose, calligraphy, and painting (Tu 1985).

Zhu Xi suggested that an exceptionally large array of ways exist in which the investigation of things can be practiced in the natural world, social relations, and the humanities (history, literature, philosophy, religion, and so forth) (de Bary 1991). In other words, for Zhu "getting it" was not simply an inner, private experience. The arts represent vehicles in which individuals can experience the joys of true learning. As stated earlier, true learning is learning that accumulates self-knowledge and brings philosophical insight into the human condition.

Regarding the things of the world, or in particular the arts, one proceeds to learn or examine them by starting from what one already knows of the principles (*li*). Then one continues to examine those principles exhaustively. After a long period of time, at some point, one can experience a breakthrough to an integral comprehension or integral consciousness (*guantong*) (de Bary and Bloom 1999). The attainment of *guantong* was said to be one of the motivating goals of Confucian learning.

Studying the arts

Development or learning takes place by reading books, through acquiring the proper actions and attitudes in determinate situations (e.g., as in ritual and social proprieties), and even through the learning of techniques and skills (e.g., music, archery, martial arts, and calligraphy). In studying the arts, once the heart-mind begins to clear and becomes quiet, one must decide what aspect of the art to concentrate on for a particular practice session (Berthong and Berthong 2000). The practitioner decides where to begin and exerts effort during the practice session.

Exhaustive study of the arts—for example, music, poetry, culinary arts, calligraphy, and medical arts—allows individuals to prune and refine their accomplishments and thereby foster their own growth and development. With respect to the medical arts, Kaptchuk (2000) explains the artistry and hierarchical nature of traditional Chinese medicine.[74] At the first level, a patient's lifestyle, symptoms, emotions, status, and environment are all considered when making a specific diagnosis. In other words, the "whole" situational context determines the patient's diagnosis and subsequent treatment.

At the second hierarchical level of diagnosis, the whole can be determined from any of the parts. For example, a highly sensitive physician can make an accurate diagnosis and discern a pattern from examining parts of the patient's lifestyle, activities, emotions, or symptoms. At this level, the whole can be determined (i.e., diagnosed) by examining any particular part, "because the whole leaves its characteristic mark on each part" (Kaptchuk 2000, 285).

At the third level of diagnosis and treatment, the physician resonates with the patient. Kaptchuk refers to this level as "an intimate, intuitive, and immediate encounter of humanity" (ibid., 288). This level of resonance with the patient is also referred to as a "Penetrating Divine Illumination" (ibid.). At this level, the physician is capable of discerning patterns (*li*) instantaneously. He or she must possess sensitive consciousness to function effectively at the third hierarchical level. At this level, the *qi* of the physician resonates with the *qi* of the patient. Divine Illumination cannot be taught; it develops within the physician as his or her craft is refined.

Hennessey (1995) describes how the *taijiquan* (*tai chi chuan*) master Zheng Manqing (Cheng Man-ching) (1902–1975) was also devoted to the exhaustive study of five classical arts: calligraphy, poetry, painting, traditional medicine, and *taijiquan*. He concludes that in studying these diverse arts, Zheng mastered one constant: the unimpeded flow of vital energy, *qi*. Hennessy notes that while it is apparent how "free-flowing energy" is critical to the study of painting, calligraphy, and *taijiquan*, the importance of *qi* is less obvious in the study and practice of poetry and medicine. However, he explains that free-flowing *qi* is also vital for cerebral arts, such as poetry and medicine, since it alleviates and mollifies

---

[74] Recall that principle or coherence (*li*) is hierarchical or holographic in nature. See chapter 3.

stagnant thought processes. Unified *qi* affects both physical and mental processes.

Similarly, Jiuan Heng discusses how calligraphy, when practiced according to tradition, facilitates the self-cultivation and transformative process. He makes clear how calligraphy can become an "art for personal expression" that integrates movement within rest, and rest within movement (2003, 26). According to Heng, "balance forms the basis of calligraphy" (ibid.).

Calligraphy, like other traditional arts, can take on an ethical dimension as practitioners cultivate themselves to undertake the discipline required to master the art. The cycle of training required to master calligraphy, as well as other arts, can be linked to the cycle required for Confucian self-cultivation, which was described in chapter 1. According to Neo-Confucian tradition, one of the outcomes of such training and self-mastery is a practitioner who spontaneously does what is right.

Recall that from the perspective of the Cheng-Zhu School, the process of learning is a process of psychospiritual transformation that refines and clarifies *qi* (Adler 2004).[75] This learning particularly influences *qi* residing in the heart-mind (*xin* or *hsin*).

Studying the arts, therefore, can provide an excellent venue for true learning, learning that accumulates self-knowledge and brings philosophical insight into the human condition. This true learning consists not only of cognitive enhancement, as principles of specific arts are better understood and more effectively applied, but also entails the acquisition of moral insights, as practitioners enhance their own moral understanding and development. Studying the arts requires methodical learning and effort over a long period of time.

However, Confucians maintained an even broader sense of art, beyond the traditional classic six arts or even more contemporary art forms. In fact, "unlike common conceptions of art that associate artworks with studios and galleries, the Confucian conception of art is the artistic way of life itself" (Ni 2008, 176). If various activities throughout life can be conceived as art, then such activities can be pursued as moral practice or *gongfu* (*kungfu*).

---

[75] See chapter 4 under the section titled "Learning of the Way and *qi*."

CHAPTER 8

The Process of *Kungfu*

Kungfu (*Gongfu*) Defined and Described

Gongfu defined

Gongfu can be defined as methodical learning over time, which requires effort (de Bary 1991; Yang 2003). An extension of the definition of *gongfu* would include "the effort spent on something, as in expressions like 'the *gongfu* of learning' and 'the *gongfu* of rectifying the heart-mind and cultivating the person'" (Ni 208, 168).[76] The term refers to moral effort or disciplined action to know and do good. Zhu Xi used "the term to describe both inward moral efforts such as adhering to faithfulness and preserving sincerity ..."; however, more typically he used the expression to refer to study and learning (Taylor 2005).[77]

Gongfu is related to the *Great Learning* through the eight steps, or processes, cited earlier in this text.[78] All eight steps lead toward the goals or objectives of learning. However, this author believes the specific steps

---

[76] "This moral practice is called *gongfu* in all three major Chinese spiritual traditions. The final goal of *gongfu* is to appropriate the ultimate universal truth and attain an experiential state of mind initially known in Buddhism as 'enlightenment' (*wu*)" (Lin 2004, 347).

[77] It is interesting to note that de Bary points out how within Japanese culture, the term *kū-fu* corresponds to the Chinese expression *gongfu*. Within the Japanese Zen tradition, *kū-fu* also implies the expenditure of effort (de Bary 1975).

[78] See chapter 3, "Confucian Learning," where the three principles and eight steps, or processes, for achieving the goals of Confucian learning are discussed.

that relate directly to *gongfu* are as follows: the investigation of things, extension of knowledge, sincerity of the will, rectification of the mind, and cultivation of personal life.

Hu Ping-wen (1250–1333) explained that while pursuing the eight steps, one does not automatically advance from one step to the next in a linear fashion. Rather, individuals are required to continually exert effort in pursuit of their *gongfu* learning (Gardner 1986). Progressing through the eight steps requires disciplined effort.

Gongfu described

Gongfu entails the acquisition of refined, or embodied, abilities. Therefore, since abilities are acquired in degrees, or levels, individuals similarly can reflect various degrees or levels of *gongfu* learning and skill (Ni 2008, 169). Perhaps the factor that distinguishes ordinary effort versus that put forth in *gongfu* is that effort in *gongfu* is *effort consciously exerted for personal transformation* (ibid). In other words, it is the intention associated with *gongfu* that distinguishes it from ordinary effort.

Learning is integral to our nature, and *gongfu* enables us to mature and make our way with the help of learning. Humankind possesses an intrinsic ability to learn, unlearn, and relearn, and to change through self-reform and self-criticism.[79] Therefore, methodical learning over time, or *gongfu*, has the potential to become true learning by impacting the inner or moral development of the learner (Gardner 1990). *Gongfu* entails true learning, learning that accumulates self-knowledge and brings philosophical insight into the human condition. It represents conscious effort exerted for personal transformation.

Wu Cheng (1249–1333), the leading Neo-Confucian scholar of the early fourteenth century, also referred to the gradual method of the sustained effort of the learning process (*gongfu*) that culminated in an experience of "integral comprehension," a state of harmony of consciousness and actions (DeBary 1991). Wu further described this acquired state as

---

[79] Such learning requires individuals to learn, unlearn, and relearn their own mental models, thereby increasing one's mental flexibility. See Young and Corzine (2004) for a business application of this transformative learning process.

one in which an individual experiences the interrelatedness of all beings and principles, a state that is inexpressible in words (ibid.).

According to Zhu Xi, when one learns over time, the proper sequence for learning, or acquiring self-knowledge, is to study extensively, inquire carefully, ponder thoroughly, sift clearly, and practice earnestly (Gardner 1990). When practicing *gongfu* methodically over time, these steps are undertaken in a continuous, cyclical manner of study, practice, and reflection. The practice of *gongfu* requires a sincere commitment.

Commitment to *gongfu*

A commitment to *gongfu* represents an unending act of self-realization (Tu 1998). One does not engage in *gongfu* to display one's own talents; rather, individuals engage in methodical learning over time out of the natural enjoyment they derive from sharing their feelings with friends and teachers who can help clarify and enhance ideas and concepts through knowledgeable discourse (de Bary 1991). Neo-Confucians felt that holding on to any "fixed" principle was an obstacle to the transcendent freedom of the mind (ibid.). Their perspective was that "principle is one but its particularizations are diverse" (Tu 1985, 138). This belief enabled them to search for and discover principles (*li*) while they learned methodically within dynamic, changing situations and contexts.[80] Zhu Xi suggested that one must have the will, or commitment, to learn over time in order to make progress in self-cultivation (Gardner 1990).

Studying the microcosmic, understanding the macrocosmic

Gongfu, when extended to its logical conclusion, suggests that achieving a larger, macrocosmic view of world ordering rests on the examination of a lesser microcosmic view of self-cultivation. This examination of a microcosmic realm, in order to better understand and function within a larger macrocosmic context, takes place over time.

In classical Chinese thought, the world is conceived as an interactive

---

[80] Young and Baker (2004) applied *gongfu* learning to the learning of entrepreneurs who start and manage growing businesses in dynamic, changing environments.

field of processes and events. Within this field, the world is continuously undergoing a process of transformation. There are no final elements of shifting "foci," or points of attention (Ames and Hall 2001). The world is interactive, dynamic, and constantly changing.

The process-oriented worldview of classical Chinese thought is made possible by the concept of *yin-yang* theory. In this theory, *yin* is always in the process of becoming its opposite, and vice versa. Hence, the Chinese world is a world of continuity, becoming, and transitoriness. "In such a world, there is no final discreteness" (ibid., 10).

In *gongfu* practice, individuals examine processes and events at the microscopic level in order to *infer by analogy* their principles (*li*) at higher macroscopic levels.[81] These higher, macroscopic levels in turn represent things that also are not discrete objects but are themselves states of becoming (Ames and Hall 2001). In other words, the "foci" (points of attention) expand and extend to the ten thousand transitory things that comprise one's field of interest. Hall and Ames (2001) refer to this perspective as a "focus" (i.e., microscopic), "field" (i.e., macroscopic) worldview. This worldview is pervasive in traditional Chinese philosophy.

In the methodical study of *gongfu,* practitioners experience a sense of self-actualization by "focusing" on specific microscopic processes within a "field" of collective human experience (Ames and Hall 2001). By focusing on the microscopic within a macroscopic environment, both the focus and the field are mutually realized, experienced, and understood (ibid., 32). For example, a *gongfu* practitioner can begin to cultivate his or her heart-mind (*xin* or *hsin*) by (1) communicating with other like-minded persons within the community, (2) developing flourishing, effective relationships, and (3) affirming one's own and supporting others' commitment to the process of self-actualization (Ames and Hall 2001).

During the process of *gongfu*, one realizes that learning is always brought back to the individual learning of the self (de Bary 1991). That is to say, the process of self-cultivation through *gongfu* rests upon a

---

[81] Recall that *li* (principle or coherence) is hierarchical or holographic in nature.

commitment to learning, a commitment of the heart-mind to "learning for one's self" (ibid., 342) or learning to improve one's self.[82]

Wang Yangming noted that individuals cannot have true knowledge unless it is put into practice (Tu 2004). Examples of this individual progress could include instances in which accomplished lute players, calligraphers, archers, charioteers, martial artists, or others internalize their skills and subsequently perform well. When *gongfu* is developed, accomplished artists internalize their skills and competencies in a manner that is fundamentally different from those who only dabble in the arts (ibid.).

Based on this understanding of individual learning and *gongfu*, Wang concluded that "genuine knowledge" reflected an embedded or internalized skill, a learned competence (Tu 2004). As such he concluded that acquiring genuine knowledge, derived from *gongfu*, represented a transformative act. Hence, according to Wang, acquiring genuine knowledge can provide an opportunity for individuals to transform their heart-minds and their nature (ibid.).

Gongfu and *li*

Chang Lü-hsiang (1611–1674) suggested that the individual practice of *gongfu* should begin with the investigation of things, or the pursuit of principle in specific instances (de Bary 1989). For example, practice of the arts creates specific opportunities for the examination of principle or coherence (*li*) while studying a particular art form. In explicit instances, *li* can be seen as patterns, logic, or the valuable, intelligible way that things fit together. The discovery and examination of *li* can be undertaken in virtually any circumstance or situation. Chang, like scholars before him, also believed that principle or coherence (*li*) was one, but its particularizations were diverse (ibid.).

Chang suggested that the process of *gongfu* could be applied to diverse things and affairs. Since things and affairs manifested diverse particularizations of coherence (*li*), these situations could be studied and examined in depth. Such an examination would be hierarchical or holographic in nature.

---

[82] Tu stated that one must make an "existential commitment" to self-cultivation or self-development (Tu 1985, 1998; Marcel 1948; Young and Corzine 2004).

He encouraged the acquisition of knowledge embodying specific principles or manifestations of coherence. Hence, the study of the arts, for example, represented especially appropriate vehicles for engaging in true learning.

Lü Liuliang (1629–1683) suggested that one should engage in learning for one's self with a perspective of vigilant self-watchfulness of the heart-mind. This perspective suggests that a reverential and respectful spirit should be maintained during the process of *gongfu*, and this spirit should be carried over into one's daily actions and thoughts (de Bary 1991). Lü Liuliang emphasized the inseparability of intellectual and moral activity. Specifically he endorsed "unceasing" active effort, which could take the form of activities such as reading, reflecting, analyzing, and weighing (ibid.). Lü also suggested the examination of principle and the search for coherence (*li*) in everyday affairs through methodical effort (*gongfu*) (ibid.). De Bary (1991, 315) quotes Lü:

> Every thing and affair has its own proper principle of what is fitting. If I can understand the proper way to deal with something, then that is its principle. If I do not understand it, I will make a mistake. Inherent in every thing and affair is its principle. The noble man, in regard to each thing and affair, seeks to make his handling of it accord with the principle of what is fitting in each case, so that they are one [integrated].

In order to progress in the effort of *gongfu*, it is essential to engage in the practice of maintaining inner mental attentiveness.

Inner Mental Attentiveness

According to Zhu Xi, a person who practiced inner mental attentiveness (*jing or ching*) possessed a mind that could more effectively "apprehend the principle in things" (Gardner 1990). *Jing* has also been translated as "reverence" (e.g., Angle 2009) and "mindfulness" (e.g., Kalton 2004).[83]

---

[83] The fact that Zhu Xi's phrase *jing* has been translated as "reverence, seriousness, or composure" demonstrates the difficulty in explaining the term in general, and

This fully attentive mind could, through a sort of resonance or sympathetic vibration, sense the principle in any wide array of things and events in the world.

Huang Kan (1152–1221), the disciple and son-in-law of Zhu Xi, stated that "abiding in reverence" was the basis of all self-cultivation. Skill at attaining *jing* is essential for the effective practice of *gongfu*. The famous Korean Confucian scholar Yi Hwang (1501–1570), better known as T'oegye, felt that *jing* was the core of Zhu Xi's teaching (Kalton 2004). By achieving *jing*, practitioners of *gongfu*, or others, could achieve the illumination of their true selves; they could also perceive the world as it is in reality in an unbiased manner. Therefore, by achieving *jing*, individuals are able to see things clearly (Gardner 2004). Zhu suggested that the mind can be fully present and balanced. However, in order to be fully present, it has to first achieve *jing* (inner mental attentiveness).

Describing *Jing*

Jing is a state in which the mind becomes absolutely attentive to whatever is before it, without any distraction (Gardner 1990).[84] Zhu derived his dual concepts of inner mental attentiveness (reverence) and the extension of knowledge from Cheng Yi (Ching 2000, 125).[85] It is the mind in a fully

---

Zhu Xi's meaning in particular (Ching 1986, 72).

[84] The contemporary scholar who researched a psychological state very similar to the Confucian state of *jing* is Mihaly Csikszentmihalyi. Summaries of his work can be found in Csikszentmihalyi (1990, 1997, and 2003). Csikszentmihalyi refers to this mental state as "flow." He describes how flow can enhance organizational performance in *Good Business: Leadership, Flow, and the Making of Meaning* (2003). Young and Logsdon (2005) also discuss how flow (differentiation) and integration (self-transcendence) can enhance the ethical and moral performance of organizations.

[85] Critics of Zhu Xi point out that the Cheng-Zhu doctrine of *jing* (inner mental attentiveness) is close to the Buddhist teaching of mindfulness (Ching 2000, 124). However, Chan (1963, 785) points out, "Neo-Confucians emphasized making an effort in handling affairs, an effort not stressed by the Zen Buddhists." Thus, in ancient classic literature *jing* only denoted composure, while the Neo-Confucians stressed making an effort in handling affairs.

concentrated state, completely in the present moment, fully responsive to the matter at hand (Gardner 2004). Cheng Yi and Zhu Xi described *jing* as the mind in a fully concentrated, focused state (ibid.). Both Cheng Yi and Zhu Xi struck a balance between *jing* (inner mental attentiveness) and *gewu* (the investigation of things) in moral cultivation (Chan 1963).

Cheng Yi and Zhu Xi felt that individuals should be mentally attentive at all times. Gardner states their position as follows:

> In greeting a parent one should be attentive, so too in reading a book, in entering a temple, in practicing quiet-sitting, in doing calligraphy, in enjoying the scenery, even in doing one's toilet. (2004, 103)

In other words, practicing *jing* is not reserved for special times or occasions. Gardner further states:

> To practice inner mental attentiveness is to sharpen the mind's alertness, to awaken it totally to the matter at hand, so that one better sees that matter as it really is (and, of course, responds to it entirely as one should). (ibid.)

The mind becomes *jing* when all of one's mental energy is focused on an object or activity.[86] When the mind achieves *jing*, one is not single-minded in the sense of tunnel vision but rather is undistracted and focused (Angle 2009). It represents single-minded focus on each matter as it arises (ibid.). Throughout his life, Zhu Xi stressed the significance of *jing* as being one of the essential activities, or elements, for developing moral cultivation (Chan 1987). He suggested that *jing*, inner mental attentiveness, "is simply the mind being its own master" (Gardner 2004, 103). Chan, who translated *jing* as "seriousness," quotes Zhu as follows: "Seriousness without fail is the way to attain equilibrium" and "For entering the Way there is nothing better than seriousness" (Chan, 1963, 601).

---

[86] Note the similarity to Csikszentmihalyi's "flow" (1990, 1997, and 2003) as referenced earlier.

Classical and Neo-Confucian perspectives

The Neo-Confucian interpretation of *jing* emphasized "a recollected and focused consciousness that became a critical factor" in Neo-Confucian theory (Kalton 2004). However, the earlier classical use and interpretation of *jing* was reverence. This reverence, emphasized in classical Confucianism, was expressed outwardly or in one's external demeanor. However, this outward expression also reflected an inward sense of self-possession and attentiveness. Therefore, the classical term *jing* was well suited for the technical meaning and nuance given to it by the Neo-Confucian scholars (ibid.).

Specifically, Zhu Xi suggested the following physical attributes for facilitating a mental state of *jing*. "The head should be upright, the eyes looking straight ahead, the feet steady, the hands respectful, the mouth quiet and composed, the bearing solemn—these are all aspects of inner mental attentiveness" (Gardner 1990, 52).

Angle translates *jing* as reverence and thus translates the exact same passage quoted above as "The head should be upright, the eyes looking straight ahead, the feet steady, the hands respectful, the mouth quiet and composed, the bearing solemn—these are all aspects of reverence" (2009, 151). Whether *jing* is translated as inner mental attentiveness or reverence, focus or concentration lies at the heart of the concept (Angle 2009).

Angle suggests that "rather than being 'full of comparisons,' the 'inner aspect' of someone advanced at reverence (inner mental attentiveness) is unified, such that one can respond to a situation without being partial to one side or the other" (2009, 154). In other words, over time the practice of inner mental attentiveness can facilitate the development of a comprehensive understanding of things, or integral consciousness (*gantong* or *kuan-t'ung*).

Ching translated *jing* as reverence and stated that it was "the process by which the original unity of the mind is preserved and made manifest in one's activity" (1986a, 280). Zhu referred to abiding in *jing* (inner mental attentiveness or reverence) and describes this state as a single-mindedness and freedom from interruption, comparing it to the Buddhist custom of mindful attentiveness (Ching 1986a).

Kalton (2004) translates this mindful alertness as mindfulness. He suggests that the concept of *jing* was developed as a method for embracing both the active and quiet aspects of self-cultivation. *Jing* allows individuals to engage in a "simple *yin-yang* like alternation between quiet and activity" (Kalton 2004, 196). From this perspective *jing*, applied properly to both the quiet and active intervals of life, becomes the fundamental nature of self-cultivation (Kalton 2004). A summary of additional characteristics of *jing* can be found in Table 8.

Table 8
Some Additional Characteristics of *Jing*

Jing can:	Achieve the illumination of one's true self Enable individuals to see things clearly
Jing	A state when the mind becomes absolutely attentive to whatever is before it. A fully concentrated, fully focused state. Completely in the present moment. Fully responsive to the matter to which one is attending. Should be present at all times. Not reserved for special occasions. Sharpens the mind's alertness.* Not tunnel vision but rather undistracted and focused. One of the fundamental activities for moral cultivation. Enables a *yin-yang* alternation between quiet and activity. The practice, over time, can facilitate the development of an integral comprehension of things, or integral consciousness.

* Similar to the Buddhist practice of mindful alertness.

Inner mental attentiveness and *li*

Zhu Xi felt that a completely tranquil mind, a mind that possessed *jing*, was a mind able to concentrate on one thing without distractions. Such a tranquil mind was essential in the quest for enlightenment (Gardner 1986). However, he also felt that the acquisition of moral knowledge, attained by probing external principles, was also essential for attaining enlightenment. It was his belief that "maintaining inner mental composure" was the foundation; however, "probing principle" (*li*) enabled that foundation to fully develop (ibid., 57).

Attaining single-mindedness and freedom from distraction is essential for the effective pursuit of *gongfu*. For example, individuals practice calligraphy, painting, music, and so forth with single-minded effort, enabling their minds to resonate with, and achieve sympathetic vibration with, the principles (*li*) contained within their chosen *gongfu* practice.

Jing and probing *li*

Probing *li* (the principle or coherence of things) and retaining inner mental attentiveness (mindfulness or reverence) are mutually interrelated. In fact, one stands little chance of apprehending the principles or coherence in things (*li*), if one's mind is biased by selfish desire or prejudice (Gardner 2004). As one examines the coherence of things, events, or affairs, one should simultaneously examine one's own feelings and reactions that are prompted by the those things, events, or affairs. One should leave the mind open in order to experience things and affairs without prejudice or preconception. Gardner (2004, 116) cites Zhu Xi as saying the following:

> The sage, in activity, is quiescent. By contrast, the multitude, in activity, is confused and disturbed. When people today want to do something, they're never capable of concentrating on it or dealing with it efficiently and without confusion. For as they deliberate on it, they want to do this and at the same time want to do that. This is why in times of activity there isn't that quiescence.[87]

For Zhu Xi, if an individual could not "preserve" his or her mind, neither would he or she be capable of investigating principles to the utmost. Therefore, he felt that there is interdependence between (1) the doctrine of inner mental attentiveness (reverence) and its need for concentration,

---

[87] This phenomenon is even more exaggerated in today's digital, virtual, and mobile society.

and (2) the concept of the extension of knowledge and the investigation of principles. Taken together, these two practices make up the formula for self-cultivation that Zhu acquired from Cheng Yi.

Gongfu, gewu, and *jing*

The Cheng-Zhu approach to self-cultivation emphasized an inch-by-inch, methodical effort to study and learning. The school's approach suggested that intense, orderly study is of great benefit to an all-inclusive and intuitive understanding of principles (*li*) (Ching 2000). The practice of *gongfu* is one approach for experiencing the interdependence of the concept of inner mental attentiveness and its need for concentration, along with the ideas of the extension of knowledge and the investigation of principles (*li*). *Gongfu* is methodical study that requires effort over time. One can engage in *gongfu* through *gewu*, the investigation of things. *Gewu* is "the process by which one may become illuminated" (Gardner 2004, 106) and can enable one to see things clearly. *Jing* is the mental attitude, or state of mind, that one brings to the process of *gongfu* (Gardner 2004). In addition to his views on inner mental attentiveness, the investigation of things, and the extension of knowledge, Zhu Xi also distinguished between lesser and greater learning.

Lesser Learning[88]

Angle (2009, 136) cites Zhu as saying, "Lesser learning is the direct understanding of a given affair." It represents the direct study of affairs and teaches one how to behave or act according to rules or accepted norms. Examples of lesser learning in general include the proper way to interact with the following individuals: one's parents; one's superior, spouse, and

---

[88] Lesser and greater learning also can be used to make the distinction between "basic curricula," geared toward children, and "more advanced curricula," developed for adults (Gardner 1986, 89). Zhu Xi made this distinction between learning for children versus learning for adults in "the educational system of the ancients" (ibid.). Learning for adults commenced at age fifteen, when students began studying—probing principle (*li*), setting the mind right, self-cultivation, and governing others (ibid., 80–81).

siblings; or one's friends. Lesser learning encompasses learning proper behaviors. It also includes learning proper actions or activities required when practicing specific types of *gongfu* (Gardner 1990). Typically, one engages in lesser learning in communal settings as practitioners begin disciplining their physical and emotional selves (Angle 2009). Within these settings, the intention for self-cultivation or self-development is aroused (ibid.).

Finally, neither Zhu Xi nor Wang Yangming saw lesser learning as a distinct step or phase that must come before greater learning. Rather, both suggested that a degree of overlap between lesser and greater learning can take place. This overlap was especially apparent during the practice of *jing*, inner mental attentiveness or reverence (Angle 2009). As individuals progressed in their *gongfu*, they matured into the practice of greater learning.

Greater Learning

Angle cites Zhu as saying, "Greater learning is the investigation of a given coherence (principle)—the reason why an affair is as it is" (2009, 136). "Greater learning illuminates the coherence behind these affairs" (ibid.). It investigates the principles or coherence (*li*) behind lesser learning. This is accomplished by scrutinizing the rationale behind the actions or activities of lesser learning. For example, after one learns the proper actions in a specific *gongfu* practice, one should deepen his or her understanding by examining the reasons behind one's actions or techniques.

Practically speaking, individuals should first master the mechanics and behaviors associated with learning a particular art form. Subsequently, after mastering these behaviors or mechanics, individuals should then deepen their learning by studying the reasons why each action or technique is as it is. In other words, greater learning represents the broadening and deepening of lesser learning (Gardner 1990). According to Angle (2009), greater learning begins when practitioners become conscious of, or develop an awareness of, their own gradual self-cultivation. As stated earlier, this self-cultivation takes place amid various relationships, and these relationships serve as an added source of motivation.[89]

---

[89] Chapter 2 describes Confucian "Self-Cultivation as a Communal Act."

In order to pursue greater learning in *gongfu*, one must build upon what he or she already knows about the matter (lesser learning). As one continues to probe a specific thing or affair, seeking to reach one's limit, the manifest and the hidden, the subtle and the obvious qualities of all things and affairs will become known.[90] The mind will become completely illuminated. Zhu Xi referred to this state as "fully apprehending the principle in things," or "the completion of knowledge" (Gardner 1990). Finally, open discussions during the processes of *gongfu* afford individuals the opportunity to confirm their learning of principles with others.

As stated earlier, methodical learning over time, learning that requires effort and energy (i.e., *gongfu*), can be applied to the study of numerous and various arts. In Part II, the application of *gongfu* to traditional Chinese martial arts will be examined.

---

[90] This is possible as a result of Cheng Yi's admonition that "Principle is one but its manifestations are many."

PART II

Applications for Traditional Chinese Martial Arts

CHAPTER 9

Principles of Traditional Chinese Martial Arts

For anything to be this thing rather than something else, it needs its own principle or pattern of order, i.e., *li* (Berthong and Berthong 2000). Pattern, principle, or coherence (*li*) are key ideas in (1) executing specific martial techniques, (2) sparring or actual combat, or (3) forms practice.[91]

In the Chinese tradition, the purpose of education always went beyond simply acquiring intellectual knowledge (Hsu 1997). In traditional Chinese society, "the long, difficult, and rigorous hours spent at school or with tutors were intended to develop not only intellectual skills but, more importantly, to foster the cultivation and refinement of character and personality" (ibid., 183). Chow and Spangler (1982) reiterate the earlier definition and discussion of *gongfu* when they explain that it represents a broad term defined as the mastery of an ability, the accomplishment, or progress toward the accomplishment, of a difficult task through highly concentrated effort. They explain that ultimately, *gongfu* implies hard work or practice, where *gong* translates as "accomplishment" and *fu* translates as "effort."

Gongfu implies training and discipline "toward the ultimate reality of the object," whether the object is the promotion of health, the cultivation

---

[91] The terms *sparring* and *combat* will be interchanged in the following discussion. Aerobic training, such as jumping rope and running, which are necessary for cardiovascular strengthening, are not covered in the discussion in this section. Nor is flexibility training, also essential for traditional Chinese martial arts, referred to in this section.

of the heart-mind (*xin* or *hsin*), or self-defense (Little 1997, 25). There are literally hundreds of styles of martial arts that have emerged and evolved from all over China (Chow and Spangler 1982). Studying and practicing martial arts represents just one of the many concrete applications of this methodical, philosophical approach to moral and personal development. Traditional martial arts, or *wushu*,[92] represents a "fine art" rather than just physical training (Little 1997). These arts can serve as vehicles that allow practitioners to become acquainted with their true selves. They can become activities that allow practitioners to learn for themselves as opposed to learning for the approval of others. Several general principles (*li*) are applicable to all traditional Chinese martial arts. Traditional *wushu* can serve as a mechanism for lesser learning, as well as greater learning as described earlier. It's ultimate objective, from a Confucian perspective, is moral development through greater learning.[93] From a traditional Confucian point of view, *wushu* masters were attempting to improve their own physical, moral, and spiritual lives.[94]

Principles and Characteristics

Traditional martial arts are considered to be acquired disciplines that build character over time (Chow and Spangler 1982). There are numerous principles (*li*) and characteristics that apply to all traditional styles of *wushu*. Master Adam Hsu outlines several guidelines that are applicable

---

[92] The term *wushu* translates as *wu* (martial) *shu* (skill or act). The special skill of *wushu* reflects the reverence the Chinese have always felt for martial arts (Kuo 1996, 1).

[93] For example, Peter Gwin (2011) describes the conflict between the basic philosophical assumptions of contemporary *wushu*, which emphasizes aerobics, fitness, and performance (lesser learning), and traditional *wushu*. Typically, greater learning is not emphasized in contemporary *wushu*. Also, Yang Jwing-ming and Jeffrey A. Bolt state that traditionally it was felt that acquiring proficiency in a given martial-arts system required at least ten years of devoted practice or *gongfu* (Yang and Bolt 1982).

[94] Excellent examples of how two historically important *wushu* masters enhanced their own moral development, over a lifetime of practice, can be found in the article "Growing Up with Wang Ziping & Madam Wang Jurong" (Wu-Monnat 1998).

to traditional martial styles (Hsu 1997). While these specific principles (*li*) and characteristics are discussed in several sources elsewhere, they are listed briefly here to demonstrate how *li* influences traditional martial arts.

These elements of *li* can be examined in a hierarchical manner. For example, practitioners of traditional *wushu*, adhering to the theoretical concepts discussed earlier in this text, search for and discover harmonious, organic unity within their own practice. Specifically, at advanced levels of training, they examine each element and hierarchical subelement of their training to ensure that each element of practice receives its due weight and consideration at the appropriate time and/or place. In other words, they examine and refine the smallest elements of their techniques and practice. Some of the principles and characteristics of traditional *wushu* include the following.

Yin-yang theory

"No aspect of Chinese civilization—whether metaphysics, medicine, government, or art"—has escaped the impact of the *yin-yang* doctrine (Chan 1963, 244). This doctrine "teaches that all things and events are products of two elements, forces, or principles: *yin*, which is negative, passive, weak, and destructive; and *yang*, which is positive, active, strong, and constructive" (ibid.). The *yin-yang* doctrine has helped to develop the traditional Chinese view that all things are related, intertwined, and that reality is a process of continual change (Chan 1963).

Zhu Xi stated the following with respect to *yin-yang* theory and the Great Ultimate: "There is no other event in the universe except *yin* and *yang* succeeding each other in an unceasing cycle. This is called Change. However, for these [this] activity and tranquility, there must be principles [*li*] which make them possible. This is the Great Ultimate" (Chan 1963, 641).[95]

The basic structure of traditional *wushu* is based on *yin-yang* theory: two mutually balancing and interdependent forces that act permanently,

---

[95] Zhu believed that the Great Ultimate contains all principles of the "five agents" as well as *yin* and *yang* (Chan 1963).

without cessation, within the universe (Little 1997). The harmonious interweaving, or interplay, of *yin* and *yang* (e.g., gentleness and firmness) is omnipresent in traditional *wushu* practice. For example, rather than opposing force with force, a practitioner in sparring can elect to complete his opponent's movements by accepting the opponent's flow of energy and borrowing the opponent's force. This approach has been referred to as the law of adaptation (ibid., 34).

Traditional Chinese martial arts never violate *yin-yang* theory. For instance, in various martial postures, *yin* and *yang* are always exhibited in the positioning of both the hands and the feet. This characteristic has a practical purpose because martial artists never know which part of their bodies they will have to use in an attack or in a defensive mode (Hsu 1997). As martial artists continue to investigate their styles exhaustively, through the process of *gewu*,[96] they become familiar with the *yin* and *yang* aspects of the various postures early in their training. And, as is the case in Chinese philosophy, the *yin* and *yang* components of the martial postures and movements change continuously.

If every thing, process, and event contains both *yin* and *yang* aspects, then the primary challenge for martial combat is to seek the *yin* aspect within an aggressor's *yang* (Chow and Spangler 1982, 28). In other words, one is challenged to find the weakness within an opponent's strength. In combat, practitioners must be able to seamlessly change their techniques and hence adjust the *yin* and *yang* aspects of various applications. In addition to the principle of *yin-yang* theory, several additional principles (*li*) can be uncovered during the study of traditional *wushu*.

Wushu techniques

Numerous principles (*li*) can be discovered and examined through the investigation of specific *wushu* techniques. *Wushu* technical advancement depends on the continued perfection of four categories of general technique. These categories are hand and body strikes, leg kicks, throws, and wrist and arm locks (which also include various holding and choking techniques) (Little 1997; Liang and He 2010). These techniques can be

---

[96] The investigation of things.

perfected through the repetition of specific individual and two-person exercises, individual and two-person forms practice, and sparring.

Ultimate perfection occurs when specific techniques are not only applied effectively but when they also become so instinctive that their use is separated from deliberate effort (Little 1997). For example, for all *wushu* techniques, the manifestation of accuracy, speed, power, body positioning, and path of delivery must be refined and perfected through practice (Lee and Uyehara 2008). In sparring or combat, the practitioner creates openings for him or herself through developed understanding of specific techniques, which in turn lead the practitioner's opponent into a dilemma (ibid.). A person is said to be proficient in *wushu* when the methods he or she utilizes are applied as if the body and limbs respond independently from the conscious mind. The techniques are applied spontaneously, without effort. When this level of skill is acquired, the skills are considered to be embedded or internalized.[97]

When pursuing *wushu* training, it's not the number of techniques practiced that is important; rather, it is how well one learns and develops specific skills that is of primary importance. It is better to know the effective application of two or three techniques than to perform a hundred techniques poorly (Little 1997). The persistent practice required to perfect *wushu* skills has the effect of transforming a martial art into a fine art. Therefore, traditional *wushu* represents the fine art of counteracting the effect of an opponent's effort and diminishing the expenditure of one's own energy (ibid.).

Additional Principles and Characteristics

Master Adam Hsu (1997) discussed several principles and characteristics that are common to all forms of traditional Chinese *wushu*. Some of the common characteristics are the use of the horse stance, the empty-leg stance, multiple use of the arms, unity of the entire body in movement, punching from the spine, use of both fists to hit a target, ability to divide

---

[97] Note how this stage of proficiency in *wushu* is intended to mirror the stage of Neo-Confucian self-cultivation in which practitioners spontaneously do the right thing in varied situational contexts.

one's attention to more than one part of one's body, keeping one's joints unlocked, coordination of both internal and external aspects and applications, incorporation of circles in all movements,[98] and multipurpose defensive and offensive movements. After delineating these numerous principles and characteristics, Master Hsu went on to outline additional basic attributes that are contained in all traditional Chinese martial-arts movements. Some of these additional essential characteristics, found in all movements, are as follows.

Basic principles (*li*) in all movements

The *head* should be held straight, and the *neck* should be relaxed. The head should be held naturally, without inclination to either side. The *eyes* should follow the movements in conjunction with the head. One should breathe through the *nose*, not the mouth. The tongue should touch the roof of the *mouth*, just behind the front teeth. One should sink his or her *shoulders*. The *back* should be straightened. *Hands* should be relaxed throughout all movements, and so forth. Master Hsu discusses these positions, as well as additional general principles for traditional martial arts, in his book *The Sword Polisher's Record* (1997). He points out that every specific traditional martial style should prescribe its own "step-by-step training program, standardized terminology, clear explanations, and correct interpretations" (Hsu 1997, 41). However, he laments the fact that such standardization is scarce, not only in traditional Chinese martial arts but also in other traditional arts, such as painting, music, Beijing Opera, and even gourmet cooking (Hsu 1997). When engaging in *wushu* practice, the roles of equilibrium and harmony become increasingly relevant

The role of equilibrium and harmony

The proficient martial artist must maintain a sense of equilibrium during sparring or combat in order to be effective. Mental turbulence or internal

---

[98] Even if movements appear to be straight punches, the fist and arm create a drilling or twisting movement toward the target (Hsu 1991, 31).

anxiety reduce coordination, slow reflexes, and hinder the precision of response (Chow and Spangler 1982). A calm mind is crucial in order to efficiently apply *wushu* techniques (ibid.). The ability to remain composed in the face of aggression requires acquired discipline on the part of the practitioner. The effective practitioner's mind is unaffected by disruptive emotional influences (Little 1997).

The conquest of agitation, by maintaining a sense of mental equilibrium, in turn enables the practitioner's actions to effectively harmonize with his or her opponent, and to prevail in the situational context. In *wushu*, one should be in harmony with, and not in opposition against, the power of one's opponent (ibid.). The practitioner harmonizes with the opponent's force by following that force until the moment when the opposing force reaches its maximum and begins to wane (ibid.). The practitioner forgets about him or herself and follows the movement of the opponent. This allows his or her mind to "remain spontaneous and ungrasped" (Little 1997, 127). Typically, when the practitioner stops to think, his or her movement and response become disturbed, and the opponent immediately strikes. Therefore, the practitioner's movements should be performed "unintentionally" without effort (ibid.).

The skilled practitioner's movement should also harmonize with the opponent's footwork. The attack or defense is based on his or her adversary's foot pattern of advancing and backing off (Lee and Uyehara 2008). By harmonizing with the opponent's foot pattern, the practitioner is able to advance or retreat just enough to facilitate a strike or a kick (ibid., 120). During this flowing, continuous, advance-and-retreat movement, the practitioner must retain both mental and physical balance.

The role of balance

During sparring, balance is important from two perspectives: one is physical and the other is emotional. When engaged in sparring, the practitioner's goal is to retain his or her balance at all times. While aiming to maintain or retain balance, he or she simultaneously attempts to break or disrupt the balance, steadiness, and equilibrium of the opponent (Chow and Spangler 1982). When the practitioner retains his or her balance during the perfect execution of a technique, the opponent will likely lose his or her balance. Therefore, in combat, imbalance leads to submission and the practice of constant balance is essential (ibid.).

Master Hsu, who was referred to earlier, also points out the importance of balance in all traditional Chinese martial arts. He explains how balance is important, for example, in terms of demonstrating roundhouse and various other kicks. He goes on to explain that balance is important in terms of implementing *yin* and *yang* postures with the feet and hands. Balance is synonymous with harmony in Chinese philosophy. Therefore, martial artists, while being watchful over their own attitudes, emotions, and motives, should strive to achieve balance or harmony in their various social relationships as well (Hsu 1997). While researching, applying, and discovering principles (*li*) is important, practitioners also attempt to continuously refine and perfect specific *wushu* techniques during practice.

Perfection through Refinements

Refinements in practice

Practitioners aim to perfect the application of their martial techniques through the ongoing improvement of their skills over time. Through the practice and enhancement of *wushu* techniques, practitioners are able to apply the method of analogical inference, transferring principles (*li*) from *wushu* practice to their daily lives. Ideally, refinements in martial-arts practice are intended to mirror fine-tuning in one's moral development. For example, as humans, our inborn moral perfection (*liangzhi*) is obscured by our impure endowment of psychophysical "stuff" (Gardner 1990). However, following Zhu Xi's approach of discovering and examining principles (*gewu*), our psychophysical stuff is gradually refined through learning. Eventually, this true learning allows one's moral perfection, innate knowledge (*liangzhi*), to be manifested. In the case of daily living, Zhu Xi suggested that "refinement" is meant to discriminate between two tendencies, selfishness and unselfishness. He suggested "refined discrimination" as an approach for holding on to the correctness of the original mind of the Way (de Bary 1989). *Wushu* practitioners make refined discriminations in the application of their techniques, discriminations that are mirrored in practitioners' own moral growth and development.[99] This refinement of techniques, which leads to the refinement of one's moral development over time, represents an application of the concept of studying the microcosmic, understanding the macrocosmic, which was discussed earlier.

In the case of those *wushu* practitioners who are consciously intent on cultivating their own moral and spiritual development over time through *gongfu*, a similar refinement process occurs.[100] As they work to continually refine their skills, they are simultaneously refining (rolling back) the psychophysical stuff that obscures their perfect innate moral knowledge (*liangzhi*). Martial artists, like all practitioners of *gongfu*, make refined discriminations continuously in their practice as they learn for themselves and thereby enhance their moral and spiritual growth. Specifically, martial artists facilitate their personal development by monitoring their own attitudes, motivations, emotions, and behavior through self-scrutiny as they practice and learn.

Gongfu requires singleness of mind over time. The earnest practice of *gongfu*, in this case martial arts, requires the continuous application of refined discriminations in practice. These refinements of physical techniques are accompanied by the monitoring of attitudes, motivation, and emotions during practice. Practitioners also become aware that they need to make ongoing objective assessments as they attempt to enhance and develop their knowledge and skill levels. Similarly, they discover that they are also required to make continuing objective evaluations of their daily lives, as they pursue their quest for personal development.

Practitioners who embark on *wushu* as a vehicle for *gongfu* learn

---

[99] *Wushu* practitioners formulate "mental models" (Norman 1983) of their skills and techniques. These mental images represent the practitioner's most recent conceptualization of how to perform a given skill or technique. Refinements through practice allow practitioners to continually revise their mental models, skills, and techniques. Such continual revisions, over time, lead to greater overall mental flexibility on the part of practitioners. See Young and Corzine (2004) for a business application of this practice.

[100] This refinement process results in the development of *wude* in Chinese martial arts. *Wude* can be defined as "martial virtue." See Wu-Monnat (1998) for two excellent examples of *wude* developed over a lifetime.

to be honest, not only with their instructors and their peers, but more importantly, honest with themselves as well. They strive to be honest in the evaluation and assessment of their own practice. Further, they must be truthful with respect to their sincerity of practice and the effort they put forth. They candidly evaluate their entire practice regimen as well as their own motives, attitudes, and emotions, as these affect their practice and ultimately their individual lives. By being forthright with themselves regarding all facets of their practice and lives, they are able to progress on the path of moral, emotional, and spiritual development. They continue to engage in their own self-watchfulness, even when they are alone (Tu 1989).

Master Adam Hsu (1997) stresses this same point. In his opinion, the most important attribute for studying traditional martial arts is that practitioners must be truthful with themselves. He feels that they should attempt to recognize and accept their own shortcomings and limitations, both emotionally and with regard to physical skills, and then strive to correct or improve such shortcomings.

As martial artists committed to moral development delve deeper into their arts, they become engaged in "broad learning, judicious inquiry, careful thought, and clear differentiation of principles" (de Bary 1989, 34). This deepening occurs as they gradually become engaged in greater learning as opposed to cursory lesser learning.

Continuous refinements

When knowledge is genuine and sincere, practice is embarked upon; when practice is clear and minutely adjusted, knowledge is present. This concept can be applied to studying and learning *wushu* principles and practices as improvements are made continuously. In Neo-Confucian learning, real or genuine knowledge and practice cannot be separated. They are united and advance together.

Genuine knowledge and practice become inseparable only after the practitioner has studied over a long period of time. In the theory of Neo-Confucian learning, when this state occurs one will instinctively respond appropriately in all social situations. Confucius, according to his own recollection, did not reach this state until the age of seventy.

Wushu provides a vehicle for practitioners to acquire genuine knowledge and true learning by inferring through analogy. For example, Zhu Xi is quoted as saying, "When one knows something but has not yet acted on it, his knowledge is still shallow. After he has experienced it, his knowledge will be increasingly clear, and his character will be different from what it was before" (Chan 1963, 609).

In the case of traditional *wushu*, after a long period of sincere study, the knowledge one attains in practice will become so embedded that the appropriate physical response will occur instinctively in any sparring or combat situation. This example illustrates again how the practice of traditional martial and other arts mirror and can serve as vehicles for one's development. In Neo-Confucian theory, genuine knowledge is practice. Similarly, from this perspective, where practice is absent there is no real knowledge (East Asian History Sourcebook 2009). As sincere *wushu* artists acquire and absorb greater conceptual knowledge, such knowledge is applied in the practice and application of their martial arts skills as they continue to refine *wushu* principles (*li*) along with their ability. Practitioners develop their skills not only by refining their techniques in specific exercises and sparring practice, but also by refining their skills through the practice of routine sequences or forms.

Continual refinement of forms

At higher levels of training, forms should be examined in depth. For instance, practitioners should take time to analyze and study their forms for relevant applications and in light of the essential principles and characteristics inherent within them (Hsu 1997). Traditional martial-arts forms consist of identifiable components that have practical uses. As the practitioner moves from one posture or technique to another, the performance of forms should be graceful (Little 1997). During the beginning (or lesser learning phase) of martial development, movements within forms usually emphasize specific postures, transitions between postures, physical conditioning, and basic training. However, as the practitioner's fundamentals improve, a major component of forms training focuses on developing practical applications of postures, transitions, and movements, in addition to the discovery of principles (*li*) (Hsu 1997).

Continual refinement of martial principles (*li*)

Practitioners continuously hone the principles contained and discovered within specific exercise, forms, and sparring practice. For example, over years of practice they enhance their understanding, application, and refinement of the general characteristics of Chinese martial arts outlined by Master Adam Hsu (Hsu 1997). As these general characteristics are polished and refined in exercise, forms, and sparring training, the practitioner's psychophysical "stuff" is gradually rolled back. This is accomplished as the practitioner continually examines his or her own attitudes, emotions, and motivations during practice sessions. As the practitioner moves from lesser to greater learning, his or her moral and spiritual development deepens, as he or she engages in continual cognitive and emotional self-scrutiny.

From the beginning of traditional martial-arts training, practitioners are encouraged to use their minds when they train (Hsu 1997). Master Hsu points out that without applying their minds, students will be unable to significantly improve their skill level, regardless of how many hours a day they train (ibid.).

Typically, as practitioners enhance their *wushu* skills over time, they develop higher-level techniques on top of their strong foundation of basic principles and characteristics. For example, as they progress from lesser to greater learning, practitioners use "less rough power," evolve "more mature techniques," and "engage the mind and spirit" (Hsu 1997, 66). They move from an external orientation toward a more internal emphasis, focusing more on vital energy (*qi*) in their martial arts (Hsu 1997). *Wushu* training then becomes a process of psychospiritual transformation that aids in refining and clarifying the practitioner's *qi*. Finally, when practitioners acquire and develop a proper learning attitude during *wushu* training, their inner strength or character is developed, along with their powers of self-confidence and concentration (*jing*) (ibid.).

As practitioners move from lesser learning to greater learning, they begin to make a deliberate commitment to the way of the sage. Neville (2000) suggests that the noted scholar Tu Weiming reports that self-cultivation is more than the outward effort toward perfection—in this case perfection through the practice of *wushu* techniques. Instead, the *gongfu* practitioner makes a conscious act of committing him or herself to the process of taking on the "identity" of one who is willing to struggle toward perfection. (ibid.)

CHAPTER 10

Learning of the Way (*Daoxue*) through *Wushu*

Earlier it was explained that the Cheng-Zhu School evolved to become the dominant, or orthodox, approach to Neo-Confucianism. Cheng Yi (1033–1107) and his brother Cheng Hao (1032–1085) had a significant impact on the concept of Neo-Confucian learning and self-cultivation. While Cheng Hao said little about the notion of the investigation of things, Cheng Yi, who had an enormous impact on Zhu Xi, made the investigation of things a major component of his philosophical system.

Since Zhu Xi, students of Cheng Yi have typically divided the process of uniting the self and *li* (principle or coherence) into two parts: internal and external cultivation. The study of traditional *wushu* can be examined from the perspective of the Cheng-Zhu School's Learning of the Way (*Daoxue*). Therefore, traditional *wushu*, through the process of *gongfu*,[101] can also be examined from the perspectives of internal and external cultivation.

Internal Cultivation

As stated previously, the internal aspect of Learning of the Way (*Daoxue*) calls for arriving at a psychophysical state of *jing*.[102] Earlier, it was

---

[101] Methodical learning over time, which requires effort and energy (de Bary 1991; Yang 2003).

[102] See Tables 4 and 8 for a description of some of the characteristics of *jing*.

explained that *jing* has been translated as inner mental attentiveness, composure, reverence, and seriousness.

During the internal-cultivation process of arriving at *jing*, *wushu* practitioners are concerned with maintaining composure, calmness, and a state of mental unity. Graham explains that this state of mental unity is "maintained by attending to only one thing at a time and fully orienting oneself toward it, without being distracted by anything else" (1992, 68).

Wushu practitioners strive to reach and maintain *jing* as they rehearse and refine their specific techniques,[103] sparring, and forms practice.[104] When *jing* is achieved, practitioners discover that the effect of this discipline and training over time is to encourage the development of some or all of the following phenomena:[105]

- Their mental activity begins to resonate with the principles (*li*) involved in the movements.
- Their will controls the flow of *qi* (vital energy).
- Pure *qi* (as opposed to turbid *qi*) comes into being.
- They begin to move into a state of goodness (moral development).

These phenomena begin to emerge when practitioners embark on the study of traditional *wushu* with the intention of personal self-development.

When practitioners make a commitment to personal self-cultivation through *wushu*, the self-improvement process requires "an existential commitment" (Tu 1995, 1998; Young and Corzine 2004) on the part of the individual.[106] In other words, the practitioner consciously commits

---

[103] Recall that the four general-technique categories are hand and body strikes, leg kicks, throws, and wrist and arm locks (which also include various holding and choking techniques) (Little, 1997,145; Liang and He 2010). Techniques can also be improved through one- or two-person exercises.

[104] Forms practice is also conducted through one- or two-person sequences.

[105] Refer to Table 4.

[106] An existential commitment represents an act, as suggested by Gabriel Marcel, in which one commits his or her entire being (1948). An existential commitment represents a change of lifestyle and a reordering of one's priorities. In order to make

to using his or her *wushu* practice as a vehicle for self-transformation and moral cultivation.

Table 8 summarizes additional characteristics of *jing* that *wushu* practitioners begin to experience when their practice is sincere. They begin to:

- achieve an illumination of their true selves and
- see things more clearly.

During practice, as *jing* is achieved, the practitioner's mind becomes absolutely attentive to what is before it. *Jing* represents a fully concentrated, fully focused state in which practitioners:

- can experience the present moment and
- are fully responsive to the matter to which they are attending.

According to the Cheng-Zhu School, this state of *jing*:

- should be present at all times and not reserved for special occasions,
- sharpens the mind's alertness,
- is not tunnel vision but rather is undistracted and focused,
- is one of the fundamental activities for moral cultivation, and
- enables a *yin-yang* alternation between quiet and activity.[107]

Over time the practice of *jing* during *wushu* practice can facilitate the development of an integral consciousness, or integral comprehension of things (*guantong*).

When *jing* is achieved through sincere practice, Neo-Confucians believe that the principle of Heaven (*tianli*) will begin to manifest itself in practitioners' lives and actions as they begin to live effortlessly, in

---

progress, practitioners of *gongfu* often make an existential commitment to their chosen paths or selected practice vehicles.

[107] This alternation between quiet and activity occurs during exercise, forms, and techniques practice as opposed to sparring or combat, although during combat, the mind should still remain in *jing*.

accordance with their true nature.[108] *Wushu* practitioners also develop their true nature on the path of Learning of the Way (*Daoxue*) through external cultivation.

External Cultivation

The external aspect of Learning of the Way (*Daoxue*) calls for extending knowledge (*zhizhi*) and the investigation of external things and affairs (*gewu*). Cheng Yi, and later Zhu Xi, felt that since various *li* (principles or coherence) were actually one *li*, it was only necessary to become fully aware of the *li* of one thing or affair to enable one to see the principle or coherence of all (Bol 1992).

With regard to the investigation and discovery of principles externally, Cheng Yi said, "In investigating things to exhaust their principles, the idea is not that one must exhaust completely everything in the world. If they are exhausted in only one matter, the rest one can *infer by analogy*'" (Graham 1992, 9–10). This same passage translated by Chan (1963, 557) reads as follows: "To investigate things in order to understand principle to the utmost does not mean that it is necessary to investigate all things in the world. One has only to investigate the principle in one thing or event to the utmost and the principle in other things or events *can then be inferred* [emphasis added]."

When *wushu* practitioners discover and examine principles exhaustively during their training, they attempt to determine why the principles they uncover are as they are (Graham 1992). For example, it was explained earlier that practitioners encounter and examine principles that include *yin-yang* theory, balance, equilibrium, harmony, and spontaneity during their training. They also practice and refine principles (instances of coherence) involving various parts of the body, including the head, eyes, shoulders, back, and hands. In all cases, they attempt not only to discover fundamental principles during their training, but more importantly, they also attempt to extend these principles to the same class of actions in different circumstances. This extension, or inferring by analogy, takes place on two levels, lesser and greater learning.

---

[108] According to Mencius, one's true nature is fundamentally good.

Lesser learning

Zhu Xi stated that lesser learning entails the direct understanding of a given event or affair (Angle 2009). It teaches one how to behave or act according to rules or accepted norms. In the case of *wushu* practice, students can become proficient in the lesser learning of their art by mimicking the actions of their teacher. One can become quite advanced in the lesser learning aspect of *wushu* by replicating the actions of one's teacher, watching visual media, and engaging in rigorous individual and partner practice. Even highly skilled, competitive *wushu* champions can be quite accomplished in lesser learning.

Inferring by analogy readily occurs during the process of lesser learning, as practitioners become skilled at refining their art and extending principles to the same class of actions in different circumstances. For example, the principles used in sweeping lotus kicks can be used in heel, spring legs, forward, hook, backward, side, and other kicking techniques (Liang and He 2010). Principles used in hand techniques can be used in elbow, throwing, seizing, knee, or body strikes, and so forth. Lesser learning involves training in proper actions and the techniques involved in executing such actions. Practitioners strive to refine and perfect their techniques in lesser learning by participating in a continuous cycle of research, practice, and refinements. Greater learning, however, takes learning to a more mature level.

Greater learning

Greater learning begins when practitioners become conscious, or develop an awareness, of their own gradual self-transformation though *wushu*. Greater learning represents the broadening and deepening of lesser learning (Gardner 1990). In greater learning, *wushu* practitioners investigate the reasons why a technique, posture, or movement is as it is. For example, practitioners can examine the reasons or rationales involved in (1) the distinct segments of *wushu* forms; (2) the hierarchical logic of techniques, movements, exercises, and forms; and (3) the finer distinctions of *wushu* actions. They examine how actions form an organic unity in technique, exercise, forms, and sparring practice. For example, body movements must be in sync with hand movements, kicks must be in sync with hand strikes and blocks, and footwork must be in sync with advances and retreats. All movements in techniques, exercises, forms, and sparring training must be implemented as a unified whole. Years of practice and fine-tuning are necessary as practitioners continue to perfect their art by discovering and examining *li* (principles or coherence) and the reasons underlying discovered *li*. In greater learning, practitioners extend *li* to their daily lives. For instance, principles such as *yin-yang* theory,[109] equilibrium, unity, and harmony, which are critical to proficient *wushu* practice, are applied to their daily lives. In greater learning, practitioners are watchful over themselves, even when they are alone.

Finally, it is important to note that lesser and greater learning are not mutually exclusive. It is not necessary for a practitioner to "complete" his or her lesser learning before embarking on greater learning. These two modes of learning are not constrained to a sequential ordering process, but instead they can occur simultaneously. As practitioners engage in both lesser and greater learning, they can infer by analogy as they study a microscopic realm in order to develop a broader, macroscopic understanding and worldview.

Studying the microcosmic, understanding the macrocosmic

In greater learning, *wushu* practitioners are fully aware of the fact that they are studying the microcosmic aspects of *wushu* with the intention of affecting, or transforming, their own worldview. They are aware of the transformative aspects of *wushu* as a legitimate form of *gongfu*. Fully cognizant of this transformative potential, they proceed in discovering *li* (principles or coherence) in practice and then, after reflection, apply such principles as *yin-yang* theory, equilibrium, balance, and harmony, and such virtues as persistence and sincerity to their daily lives. Practitioners of greater learning realize that in the process of perfecting their *wushu,* they are simultaneously enhancing their own moral and

---

[109] For example, an understanding of *yin-yang* theory suggests an appreciation and understanding of the concept of the mutual entailment of opposites in one's *wushu* practice, as well as in one's daily life (e.g., Ames and Hall 2003, 27–29).

spiritual development. They practice with the understanding that, over time, they will improve themselves based on their commitment to improving their heart-mind (*xin* or *hsin*).

Li (principles or coherence) are discovered in *wushu* training both *deductively* and *inductively*. For instance, practitioners can begin with preconceived principles such as harmony, balance, equilibrium, *yin-yang* theory, wholeness, spontaneity, unity, and change, and then they can look for hierarchical examples of various principles within their practice. This method would represent a deductive approach to inquiry.[110] Or practitioners could instead practice and discover various classical examples of coherence, an inductive approach.[111] Zhu Xi recognized the value of both deductive and inductive approaches to practical inquiry (Chan 1963, 591).[112]

Similarly, *li* can be apprehended, or understood, by practitioners *objectively* and/or *intuitively*. Objective understanding of classical concepts occurs when individuals logically observe various principles during their practice. They knowingly observe the study or discovery of classical principles. Intuitive understanding occurs when practitioners acquire a direct perception of principles without any obvious or recognized reasoning process. *Wushu* practitioners acquire an intuitive understanding of principles when they experience sudden learning breakthroughs and/or realizations of principles (*li*) without obvious preliminary learning steps or sequential reasoning. They experience aha moments in their understanding. The role of discussion figures prominently in the process of Learning of the Way (*Daoxue*) through *wushu* and is discussed next.

---

[110] This deductive approach represents a top-down method for examining principles (*li*). Practitioners begin with preconceived principles and work their way "down" to specific examples of the principles within their practice.

[111] Utilizing an inductive approach, practitioners can move from specific observations to the realization of broad principles (*li*). In this "bottom-up" methodology, practitioners recognize patterns, or instances of coherence, and subsequently come to the conclusion that such patterns represent general classical principles (*li*). Neo-Confucian philosophy looks for patterns through the practice of *gewu*. Zhu Xi recognized both the inductive and deductive approaches to inquiry (Chan 1963, 591).

[112] See Table 6.

The Role of Discussion

Like all Chinese *gongfu*, learning through discussion is of particular importance when studying traditional martial arts. Confucians feel that in learning there is no understanding without discussion (de Bary and Bloom 1999). Teachers and friends help clarify one's thinking by talking things out (ibid.). As Confucius said, there was great "joy in having friends come from afar" to share their learning and aid in each other's cultivation (ibid.).

Discussions—either in formal martial-arts classes or through informal conversations—serve as a means of confirming in others the experiences, insights, and understandings that would otherwise be merely one's own subjective opinion. Traditional *wushu* represents a learning modality in which students learn through conversations with others. In these settings, teachers and fellow students aid one another in clarifying their thinking by talking things out (DeBary 1991). Practicing the arts (in this case the martial arts) allows individuals to engage in self-questioning, self-answering, self-proclaiming, and self-confirming processes (ibid.). All of these processes are essential for self-cultivation through learning.

When studying *wushu*, discussion with others allows students and instructors opportunities to examine difficulties, setbacks, breakthroughs, and insights. Such conversations allow individuals to develop cognitively[113] and emotionally as they refine their practice and techniques.

Practicing traditional *wushu* over an extended period of time, continually making refinements in one's practice, can eventually lead to a comprehensive understanding of one's contextual situation. Master Hsu (1997) referred to this comprehensive understanding, or integral consciousness, as "global awareness" for *wushu* practitioners. In this state of alertness, practitioners become aware of their global environment and ensure that their surroundings serve their practice or sparring needs. This global awareness represents "a state of mind and ability that can only be reached through hard work and an open attitude" (Hsu 1997, 131). It represents a domain in which one's focused awareness spans

---

[113] Cognitive development includes learning new martial skills and refining existing skills.

several directions simultaneously (Hsu 1997). It entails a comprehensive understanding of one's situation, a state of "integral consciousness"[114] (e.g., Gebser 1985; Combs 1996; Young and Logsdon 2005).[115]

The Role of Inquiry

Exhaustive inquiry

Referring once again to Zhu Xi, if "to investigate things is to discover exhaustively that this event ought to be done in this way and that event ought to be done that way" (Lee 1987, 26), then various principles (*li*) are sought and examined exhaustively in martial-arts practice. Such principles, or normative standards, are examined in performing various choreographed routines, as well as in actual combat.

Lü Liuliang (1629–1683), a spokesperson for the orthodox Neo-Confucian revival, considered moral principle "natural" and advocated "unceasing" study for advancement in the Way. He emphasized the need to study, learn, and practice (DeBary 1991). Wushu practitioners committed to moral development continually research all aspects of their art. This exhaustive inquiry relies on all forms of research, including discussion with teachers and peers, the examination of articles and texts, as well as researching all forms of digital multimedia.

Processes and methods of inquiry

In traditional *wushu*, one can experience the benefits of Confucian learning by engaging in various inquiry processes. For example, in studying a particular martial style, the practitioner can engage in activities, such as broad learning, judicious inquiry, thorough pondering,

---

[114] This state of comprehensive awareness, of one's environment and one's particular place within it, is referred to as a focus/field awareness and is pervasive within traditional Chinese philosophy (see e.g., Ames and Hall 2001, 2003).

[115] See chapter 1, footnote 7, for a description of integral consciousness, or "wholistic consciousness" by several more contemporary scholars.

careful discrimination, and earnest practice—all of which, according to Confucians, are processes for experiencing the Way (de Bary and Bloom 1999).

Learning represents a process by which one corrects one's mind. If understanding moral principle is achieved through the investigation of things and affairs, then *wushu* represents one vehicle for conducting such an investigation. This can be achieved by studying a particular martial style and continually refining one's own practice. Studying *wushu* can represent a viable vehicle for discovering and investigating specific principles. Traditional Chinese martial arts represent excellent vehicles for enabling one to engage in self-examination and self-correction, allowing individuals to employ learning, unlearning, and relearning. Before concluding this examination of Learning of the Way, a brief discussion of Confucian *qigong* and quiet sitting meditation practices is in order.

CHAPTER 11

Confucian Practices and Legacy

This chapter briefly discusses two important Confucian practices, as well as the Confucian legacy from the Qing Dynasty to the present day. Two important practices are Confucian *qigong* meditation and Confucian quiet sitting meditation.

Qigong and Quiet Sitting

Confucian *qigong* meditation

Qi is the intrinsic substance, or vital force, behind all things in the universe (Liang and Wu 1997). Generally speaking, *qigong* refers to any set of breathing and *qi* (vital energy) circulation techniques that are capable of improving physical and mental health, preventing illness, and strengthening the body (ibid.). *Qigong* is a process of training the mind, body, and spirit with the objective of guiding one's thoughts in order to prepare for further development.

All traditional *wushu* grandmasters employed martial *qigong*, to a greater or lesser extent, to augment their actual fighting techniques. Confucian scholars though did not create *qigong* forms and exercises to the same extent as Taoist and Buddhist scholars (Liu 2010). However, since *qigong* aims to transmute turbid (i.e., opaque or cloudy) *qi* within the mind and body into clear, refined *qi*, the entire Neo-Confucian process of self-cultivation practice can be viewed as a *qi*-clarification process (Ni 1996).

The traditional Confucian transformation model starts with

individual meditation and moves through personal enhancement, self-discipline, personal integrity, family integration, and state governance, and reaches the level of universal commonwealth. Historically, Confucian *qigong* practice was considered of great importance. While Confucians created relatively fewer treatises on *qigong* and fewer distinctive *qigong* forms compared to the Daoists and Buddhists, there is a record of Zhu Xi "observing the breath" and citing the benefits of this practice for health (Liu 2010, 119).

During the Song Dynasty (960–1279), Neo-Confucian scholars advocated self-cultivation through the practice of meditation, breath control, and internal alchemy in order to cultivate social harmony and political correctness (Reid 1998). They felt that by promoting *qiqong*, individuals would become healthier and more useful and productive members of society. This was because, they believed, a peaceful, orderly state of mind served as the basis of a peaceful, orderly society (ibid.). The basic goal of Confucian *qigong* meditation is the desire to reach a peaceful state so one can become a thoughtful, moral person in his or her interactions with others. In addition to the practice of various forms of *qigong* to calm the body, mind, and spirit, practitioners also engaged in Confucian quiet sitting meditation.

Confucian quiet sitting meditation, or *jingzuo* (*ching-tso*)

Traditional *wushu* grandmasters could engage in quiet sitting to calm their minds and therefore avoid physical conflict completely or prevail during actual combat. It was after Confucianism responded to the popularity of Buddhism and Daoism when Neo-Confucians added quiet sitting as an aid to self-cultivation. Quiet sitting was a technique that calmed both the body and the mind in order to achieve a composure that could be sustained in action (de Bary 1975).[116] Hence, both Taoist and Chan Buddhist forms of meditation influenced *jingzuo*, or quiet sitting.

---

[116] Typically, Neo-Confucian quiet sitting was practiced either in one's home or study as opposed to a practice in a separate meditation hall or temple, which frequently occurred in Buddhist practice. In the case of Confucian schools, separate meditation halls were absent (de Bary 1975, 172).

However, unlike Chan (Buddhist) meditation, quiet sitting was never aimed at clearing the mind of conceptual thinking (Keenan 2011). This form of Confucian meditation is important because it teaches the practitioner many things having to do with one's self, including self-awareness, self-enhancement, self-discipline, and self-actualization, as well as how to find the truth and create social change. A main focus of these meditations is to incorporate body, mind, and spirit for physical healing, with the three main goals of preventing disease, promoting health, and developing human capacity.

The goal of Confucian quiet sitting meditation was to let the heart-mind (*xin* or *hsin*) become tranquil, to dwell in a quiet mode so the heart-mind could be scrutinized in terms of its basic nature (Berthong and Berthong 2000). An unrestrained and distracted heart-mind would certainly be out of touch with both external and internal principle (*li*) (Kalton 2004). Therefore, the objective of quiet sitting was to achieve a quiet heart-mind that in turn aided one's capacity for comprehension and understanding (Berthong and Berthong 2000). For example, Zhu Xi urged his students to participate in *jingzuo*, quiet sitting, in order to achieve a clear, settled state of mind that could render an undistorted, active response to external stimuli. On one occasion, he even suggested a regime of spending a half day in quiet sitting and the other half reading the Four Books[117] (Gardner 1990).

Zhou Dunyi (Chou Tun-i)[118] (1017–1073) and the Cheng brothers all practiced quiet sitting. However, Zhu Xi made a special effort to show how Confucian quiet sitting differed from Daoist and Buddhist meditation (Ching 2000). Zhu regarded meditation as a means toward an end rather than an end in itself (ibid.). He felt that meditation was a time when an individual filled his or her heart-mind with principles of right action in order to facilitate a disposition of inner mental attentiveness (*jing*) that could permeate one's entire life. He disapproved of self-ab-

---

[117] The Four Books were the *Analects*, the *Mencius*, the *Great Learning*, and the *Doctrine of the Mean*.

[118] As mentioned in chapter 4, Zhou Dunyi was one of Zhu Xi's intellectual mentors. He suggested that humans can master their *qi* (vital energy) in order to accord with nature.

sorption through meditation or quiet sitting (ibid.). Zhu advised against spending too much time sitting quietly and reflecting (meditating), and suggested that individuals should find a balance in their lives where they would study and reflect upon what they study, in equal measure.

Zhu's view of the relative importance of quiet sitting (stillness and tranquility) evolved over time. In his earlier life (before he was thirty-nine), he emphasized stillness and tranquility. Later, after age thirty-nine, he preferred inner mental attentiveness or reverence (*jing*) because it could be practiced in both activity and tranquility (ibid.). In other words, he proposed a doctrine of moral and spiritual attentiveness over oneself, accompanied and strengthened by the acquisition of knowledge (the investigation of things) about oneself and the world (ibid.).

Confucians practiced *jingzuo* as an aid to self-improvement to enhance virtues and eliminate vices (Ching 1986b). By stilling the heart-mind in quiet sitting, a person could take stock of his or her life and see what further effort was needed, what additional insights were required, and what other study was appropriate (Berthong and Berthong 2000). The primary intention in quiet sitting was to calm the heart-mind enough to be able to reflect on the spiritual aspects of ordinary life (ibid.).

Jingzuo's is understood to complement Zhu Xi's dictum to "investigate things" in order to penetrate the principle (*li*) of the cosmos. For Zhu, *jingzuo* did not mean to sit still, "with the ear hearing nothing, the eye seeing nothing, and the mind thinking nothing" (Yao 2000, 220). In contrast, it aided individuals in actively searching out, investigating, and exploring the world in which they lived.

Wang Yangming also did not want quiet sitting to be his students' only practice. He felt that the practice was only worthwhile if it could help his students grow in virtue and learn/reflect on how they, as moral persons, should grow.

Li Yung (1627–1705), considered a "neo-orthodox" Confucian scholar, advocated quiet sitting as a prelude to and preparation for action. He, too, did not suggest the practice as an end in itself (de Bary 1989). Instead he felt the practice should focus on the quiet state of mind that is present before emotions are aroused. In his opinion, the benefits of the practice accumulate over time for both individuals and for society as a whole (ibid.).

Next, a brief discussion of the legacy of Confucianism, from the Qing Dynasty to contemporary times, is considered.

Qing (Ch'ing) Dynasty (1644 –1912)

China's last three dynasties, the Yuan or Mongol (1279–1368), Ming (1368–1644), and Qing or Manchu (1644–1912), all endorsed the Cheng-Zhu School of Neo-Confucianism as the orthodox approach for preparing for the civil service examination (Keenan, 2011).[119] There was relative continuity of influence of the Cheng-Zhu orthodox approach into the early twentieth century (Munro, 2008). This meant that from the fourteenth century (1313) to the twentieth century (1905), the Learning of the Way (*Daoxue*) interpretation of the classics was officially sponsored in China.

In the Qing Dynasty, there was a scholarly and official reaffirmation of Zhu Xi's orthodox teachings. This official reaffirmation had a significant influence on the practice of *gongfu* in general and, hence, on the performance of *gongfu* through traditional *wushu* training. The concept of learning was expanded to include all kinds of learning, and the notion of true learning developed to encompass virtually every kind of human endeavor—including the study of the classics (de Bary 1991). De Bary states that during this period, the thought of one actually achieving the breadth and balance of Zhu Xi was still an honored ideal. But the actualization of such a balance and depth was "as far removed from practical realization as the ideal of the Renaissance man became for twentieth-century man in the West" (ibid., 362).

During this dynasty, there arose a whole new attitude toward the study of the Confucian Way, known as "evidential research" (Berthong and Berthong 2000, 103). This trend toward practical learning and evidential inquiry began early in the Qing Dynasty. The School of Evidential Research, also referred to as the School of Han Learning, was particularly influential in the eighteenth and early nineteenth centuries (de Bary 1989).

---

[119] As far back as the Northern Song Dynasty (960–1127), the government began to establish some government-run schools. Even during the Ming Dynasty (1368–1644) and the prominence of private schools, private schools often took as their model the curriculum utilized in state schools (Munro 2008, 103).

The most influential scholar of the Qing Dynasty was Dai Zhen (Tai Chen) (1724–1777). He was a prominent advocate of the "investigations based on evidence" approach to scholarship (Chan 1963, 709). For Dai, principle (*li*) encompassed only the order of things and affairs. He advocated examining principle by way of a "critical, analytical, minutely detailed, and objective study of things" (ibid., 710). Chan cites Dai as saying, "*Li* is a name given to the examination of the minutest details which make necessary distinctions. This is why it is called the principle of differentiation" (ibid., 711). It is reasonable to assume that this approach to the investigation of things (*gewu*), through the examination of the minutest details of *li* (principle or coherence) was adhered to by *gongfu* practitioners of the period. Traditional *wushu* practitioners would have been (and continue to be) influenced by this approach when they refined their techniques. Dai believed that principle (*li*) was only valid if it could be substantiated by "many generations" throughout the world (Fung 1983).

Between 1895 and 1911, law mandated that Confucian private schools transition to contemporary public schools. Typically, the training that had previously focused on self-cultivation became new "ethics" courses in public schools (Keenan 2011, 94). By the end of the nineteenth century, greater emphasis was placed on the importance of social interaction, or interpersonal relationships, in Confucian practice. Social interaction was viewed as a moral practice and spiritual exercise, as practitioners were challenged to put themselves in the place of the other person before taking action (Keenan 2011). Practitioners believed that the more they put themselves in the place of another, the stronger their empathy, and consequently their humaneness, would become.

The Qing scholars asked, "Why and what do we study?" They felt that a real Confucian was a person who examined reality in order to serve other human beings. Hence, scholars needed to return to solid historical, philosophical, and scientific studies. They also argued for the need to return to the study of the earliest versions of the extant Confucian classics, as well as the need to return to the study of history and other practical sciences. During this dynasty, the Confucian tradition saw a surge of educated men and women seeking to realize the Way in their own lives in service to others (Berthong and Berthong 2000). In the late Qing Dynasty, the scholar Kang Youwei (K'ang Yu-wei) (1858–1927) and others pushed for radical reform within the Confucian framework. However, this effort was unsuccessful, and the dynasty fell in 1912 (Liu 2004). In the early twentieth century it was not uncommon to blame the Confucian tradition for the dynasty's collapse.

New Confucianism (1912–Present)

From the perspective of New Confucianism, also referred to as Contemporary Neo-Confucianism, there are three epochs of Confucian philosophy (Liu 2004). First is the classical period of Confucius (551–479 BCE) and Mencius (371–289 BCE). Second is the Neo-Confucian period, which emerged during the Song–Ming dynasties. This period was created to answer the challenges from Buddhism and Neo-Daoism (ibid.).[120] Third is the period of New Confucianism or Contemporary Neo-Confucianism. These scholars see their role as developing a new philosophy that will respond to significant cultural challenges from the West (Liu 2004).

After the fall of the Qing Dynasty in 1912, the "new culture" movement emerged in China. This was symbolized by the May Fourth Movement of 1919.[121] The new culture movement saw an upsurge in nationalism and a move toward a populist base rather than intellectual elites. What had allowed China, and in fact East Asia, to become a society of ritual and music was now faulted as the source of backwardness in the Chinese economy, politics, society, and culture (Tu 1986). This movement away from cultural tradition continued under the official ideology of Marxism-Leninism-Maoism. Finally, the climax of the anti-Confucian campaign reached its apex during the Cultural Revolution, which took place from 1966 to 1977. The brief historical synopsis presented here will help explain why the majority of contemporary *wushu* practitioners, in

---

[120] During this period, Confucianism spread to Korea, Japan, and Vietnam (Tu 1993, 149).

[121] The May Fourth Movement is named after a demonstration of between 3,000 and 5,000 university students in Beijing who protested foreign intervention, as well as Chinese warlords. The term *new culture movement* refers to the period between 1915 and 1921.

China and abroad, see no connection between the art they practice and the centuries-old Confucian tradition.

However, several New Confucian scholars have continued to emphasize the link between Neo-Confucian philosophy and modern practice. New Confucians, or Contemporary Neo-Confucians "differ among themselves in their understanding of the implications of Confucianism and their reconstructions of Confucianism as a system of philosophy" (Li 2003, 716). New Confucianism, which represents a third period of Confucian humanism, has been addressed by scholars such as Mou Zongsan, Tang Junyi, Xu Fuguan, and Tu Weiming (e.g., Tu 1986).[122] Mou Zongsan (1909–1995), for example, is acknowledged as one of the most insightful Confucian thinkers of the twentieth century (Lin 2004). He advocated moral practice, or *gongfu*. However, he disagreed with Zhu Xi that achieving an enlightened state could be attained by continually "investigating things" (ibid). He felt that enlightenment could be achieved by extending one's *liangzhi* (innate knowledge or primordial awareness of good[123]). He believed that enlightenment could be attained through *shendu*, "being watchful over oneself when alone" or "vigilant solitariness." Mou felt that Confucian ethics should be rooted in "concern consciousness" (Berthong 2010). Concern consciousness reflects a constant, vigilant concern for self, family, community, society, nation, the world, and beyond (ibid.).

Another prominent New Confucian is Tang Junyi (1909–1978). Tang was born in Yibin, Sichuan Province, China. He, along with Mou Zongsan, Zhang Junmai, and Xu Fuguan, drafted the famous manifesto on Chinese culture, which was signed by these four scholars on New Year's Day 1958. This essay, "A Declaration of Chinese Culture to the Scholars of the World," states the authors' concerns regarding the general direction of human culture and the value that Chinese culture could provide to the overall development of humankind.[124] The essay marked

---

[122] The first two periods are the classical era of Confucius and Mencius, and the Neo-Confucian period that commenced during the Song Dynasty and ended after the Qing Dynasty.

[123] Every human possesses this innate, primordial awareness at a deep level.

[124] This essay was published simultaneously in two Hong Kong journals, *Minzhu pinglun (Democratic Tribune)* and *Zaisheng (Renaissance)* (Makeham 2003, 27).

the official birth of contemporary New Confucianism in Hong Kong, Taiwan, and overseas (Liu 2004).

According to Tang, the individual mind is capable of reaching nine "worlds" (ibid.). These nine worlds, or perspectives of consciousness, can in turn be grouped into three perspectives, or categories, of consciousness. These three categorical levels are (1) the worlds of the object or "objective" perspective, (2) the worlds of the subject or "subjective" perspective, and (3) the worlds that transcend both the subject and the object.[125] He advocated the attainment of a transcendent aspect of one's experience that enables individuals to become better persons in a moral sense (Ng 2004), and he stressed that the process of moral and spiritual awakening is a self-driven effort (ibid.). Finally, Tang felt that the perfection of one's self is not only a process of fulfilling one's self but also a process of fulfilling others (ibid.).

The last New Confucian scholar to be reviewed here is Tu Weiming (1940 to present). Tu was born in Kumin, Yunnan Province, and graduated from Tunghai University in Taiwan before going to Harvard, where he earned his Ph.D. He feels that Confucianism has three important ingredients: Dao, xue (hsueh) (learning), and cheng (politics) (Liu 2003). Like the prominent Neo-Confucian scholars who preceded him, Tu makes it clear that the way of the sage is not only a matter of personal cultivation but also entails the cultivation of one's relationships (Neville 2000). Tu has become a great proponent of Confucian philosophy and values in the United States. He develops the idea of a fiduciary society as an alternative to contemporary Western society's emphasis on solitary interests, which typically places too much emphasis on competition (Liu 2003). He has promoted the idea of "cultural China" and feels that many Confucian values can be appropriated by other faiths. Tu believes that Confucianism is open to the world and its values can be practiced by anyone, of any culture, who is willing to implement them in his or her life (ibid.).

---

[125] It should be noted that Tang's three worlds are similar to the three generic levels of consciousness advocated by contemporary noetic-science researchers in the West; e.g., see Wilber (1999) for an extensive comparison of multiple models of levels of consciousness. Also see Young and Logsdon (2005) for a description of the first stage, or level, of postconventional consciousness. This first level of postconventional consciousness is similar to guantong. See footnote 6 in chapter 1.

Figure 1 depicts the "concentric circles" of relationships found in traditional Confucian philosophy. Tu suggests that learning to be human entails learning to be sensitive to an ever-expanding network of relationships as shown in Figure 1 below (Tu 1985, 175). He states that this expanding sensitivity represents a consciousness-raising activity, a process of broadening the self (Tu 1985). In a similar manner, the Cheng-Chu School of thought suggested that the moral development of individuals is a conscious-raising activity that involves "overcoming the unclarity of the mind" that accompanies the "indulgence of 'selfish human desires'" (Bloom 1985, 311). For example, Zhu Xi suggested a level of consciousness that leads to a universal altruism, an ideal that requires the mutual cultivation of empathy and knowledge concurrently (Munro 2005). Similarly, we can also say that the process of *gongfu*, through traditional *wushu*, can likewise be conceived as a consciousness-raising activity as depicted in Figure 1.

Figure 1
The Broadening Process of the Self

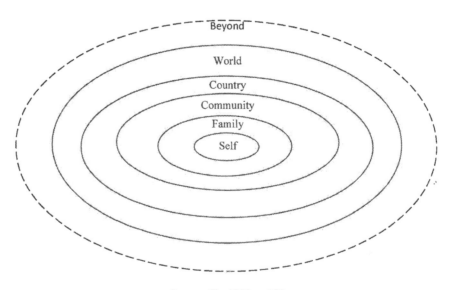

Source: Tu, 1985, p. 175.

CHAPTER 12

Conclusion

Raising Consciousness through *Wushu*

Neo-Confucians felt that a comprehensive understanding of situational contexts, which developed character and practical judgment in daily life, was realistically attainable through the diligent practice of various methods of *gongfu*, or effort. Traditional wushu artists embarked upon this consciousness-raising endeavor through the practice of their selected *wushu* system. Consciousness-raising commenced when practitioners became aware of their own gradual self-transformation, which was referred to as greater learning (Angle 2009).

It was suggested earlier that the goal of Confucian self-cultivation was, and is, to strive for human moral perfectibility through self-effort. Confucians attempt to achieve this goal through learning, where *true learning* is defined as learning that enhances one's character and practical judgment. Over time this learning develops one's inborn capacity for feeling and understanding. Confucians believe that a desire to learn, and an ability to enjoy true learning, is inherent in human beings (Gotshalk 1999).[126] It was proposed that the product of successful Neo-Confucian learning is an individual capable of instinctively seeing, or intuiting, the potential harmonious patterns in daily life (Bol 2008). Such instinctive discernment is facilitated when individuals attain a state of integral con-

---

[126] Chapter 1, verse 1, of the *Analects* presents the following quote by Confucius: "To learn, and then, in its due season, put what you have learned into practice—isn't that still a great pleasure?" (Hinton 1998). Or "Is it not pleasant to learn with a constant perseverance and application?" (Legge 1971).

sciousness, or what Confucians referred to as a "comprehensive understanding" of situational contexts, or *guantong*. *Guantong*, consciousness raising, *gongfu*, and *wushu*, as well as the efforts of New Confucians, are discussed next.

Guantong

This text underscores the importance of the concept of *guantong* (integral consciousness or the comprehensive understanding of situational contexts) in Neo-Confucian thought and scholarship (de Bary 1991). Neo-Confucians felt that when individuals achieved *guantong*, they would be better able to engage in more objective problem-solving and more successful development of meaningful social relationships. They were better equipped to make moral decisions, and they acquired an improved capacity for effectively distinguishing right from wrong. According to Confucian philosophy, this capability, or level of consciousness, developed after self-cultivation over a long period of time, allows the Principle of Heaven (*tianli*) to manifest itself within the minds and actions of individuals.[127] Achieving *guantong* allows individuals to attain greater impartiality. And, as noted earlier, Zhu Xi stated, "Impartiality, altruism, and love are all descriptions of *ren* [goodness, humanity, humaneness]. Impartiality is antecedent to *ren*; altruism and love are subsequent. This is so because impartiality makes *ren* possible, and *ren* makes love and altruism possible" (Chan 1963, 633). Individuals attained *guantong* by raising, or expanding, their own personal levels of consciousness.

Raising, or expanding, consciousness

The Confucian consciousness-expanding process, depicted in Figure 1, is in line with the notion of a perennial philosophy that has been articulated on numerous occasions in Western philosophy. The concept of a perennial philosophy can be traced as far back as the Platonic-Christian

---

[127] See footnote 7 in chapter 1 for a list of contemporary Western philosophers and scholars who have also described and cited the spiritual and practical benefits of integral consciousness.

synthesis of St. Augustine (Young 2002), while the expression "perennial philosophy" itself was first used during the Renaissance (Loemker 1973).[128] The single conviction that runs through the perennial philosophy is the belief that Absolute Spirit, Pure Consciousness, Universal Mind—or as the Neo-Confucians believed, the Principle of Heaven (*tianli*), *Taiji,* or Supreme Ultimate—is the fundamental essence of human nature and the totality of reality.[129]

This element or truth can be found at the heart of the mystical teachings of all of the world's religious traditions and philosophies (Ferrer 2000). This potential for the hierarchical understanding and experience of being suggests that knowledge obtained through the higher realms is more essential, reveals more about reality, and is therefore more authoritative and authentic than knowledge obtained through the lower realms or perspectives of understanding (Young 2002). As individuals alter their sense of identity, moving from selfish egocentrism to more unselfish universal perspectives, this is what Wilber has referred to as transformative spirituality, or transformative spiritual practice (2000).

From the perspective illustrated in Figure 1, true knowledge—obtained as practitioners move from the cultivation of the self to perceptions encompassing broader, less egocentric worldviews—will be more authentic than true knowledge obtained at the earlier stages of learning.[130] Enlarging one's perspective, moving from the self (see Figure 1) to an appreciation of and empathy for the world and beyond, represents a process of moral development similar to the process described by American psychologist Lawrence Kohlberg (Kohlberg 1986). Confucians, like contemporary Western psychologists concerned with adult ego development,[131] describe a framework of moral development that culmi-

---

[128] Aldous Huxley popularized this concept in his 1945 publication *The Perennial Philosophy.*

[129] Recall Cheng Yi's admonition that "principle is one but its manifestations are many" (Chan 1963, 544).

[130] The New Confucian scholar Tang Junyi (1909–1978) suggested nine hierarchical levels of consciousness, which he referred to as nine "worlds" or perspectives.

[131] From the Confucian perspective, adult ego development began at the age of fifteen as individuals moved through the Confucian life cycle. See the *Analects,*

nates in a universal morality (Kohlberg and Ryncarz 1990). From the Confucian perspective, this adult moral development can only take place by, or through, sustained effort over time, defined as *gongfu*.

Gongfu and wushu

Neo-Confucians emphasized expanding consciousness through *gongfu*. The methodology that emerged as the orthodox approach to *gongfu* stressed the investigation of things (*gewu*), practiced by the Cheng-Zhu School. This approach was the dominant form of Confucian practice at the time of the fall of the Qing Dynasty in 1911.[132] This text has examined the practice of *gongfu*, the quest for moral perfectibility through the sustained practice, study, and perfection of *wushu* (martial arts).

The book has attempted to explain the Confucian philosophical principles that underlie the practice of *wushu*. While there have been some attempts to examine the Confucian foundation of *wushu* (e.g., Hennessy 1995), typically the philosophical underpinnings of *wushu* are not well understood nor thoroughly examined in either China or the West. This book has also attempted to describe the Confucian foundation that supports the practice of *gongfu* through traditional *wushu*. In the process of delineating and describing the Neo-Confucian principles of traditional *wushu*, the text has shown that several Confucian principles have universal appeal. These universal principles are emphasized by the most recent intellectual movement of Confucian scholarship, New Confucianism.

New Confucianism

The text briefly examined the New Confucian movement. One of the most prominent proclamations of New Confucianism was the 1958

---

chapter 2, verse 4, for Confucius's description of the stages of his own adult ego and moral development (e.g., see Hall and Ames 1987).

[132] However, Chan Buddhism was the dominant religious practice at the time of the fall of the Qing Dynasty. The Chinese Revolution of 1911 ended with the abdication of the emperor on February 12, 1912.

publication of an essay titled "A Declaration of Chinese Culture to the Scholars of the World." As stated earlier, this essay presented its authors' concerns about the general direction of human culture and the value that traditional Chinese culture could provide to the overall development of humankind. Following this line of reasoning, two of the most prominent contemporary scholars responsible for introducing Confucian concepts to the West have been Professors Tu We-ming of Peking University and Harvard, and William Theodore de Bary of Columbia University, both of whom have been cited extensively here.[133] It appears that the time to explore Confucian concepts and practices, as well as other traditional Chinese philosophical ideas, in contemporary scientific settings has arrived. Some thoughts for future research on traditional Neo-Confucian practices are presented next.

Future Research

It is suggested here that a vast array of future research could be conducted on the efficacy of Neo-Confucian principles and practices and the impact these practices have on successful daily living and society. For example, case studies of various Neo-Confucian practices could be examined.

Single-case studies

In a sense, this manuscript can be contextualized as a preliminary single-case study (Miles and Huberman 1994; Miles, Huberman, and Saldaña 2014) exploring the discovery and application of Confucian and Chinese concepts within the context of traditional *wushu*. However, as pointed out by Chow and Spangler (1982), martial-arts historians propose that there are approximately 360 traditional Chinese *wushu* systems. These systems can be further subdivided into schools and branches. For instance, external hard styles versus internal soft styles (e.g., Reid and Croucher 1983) can be examined. In addition, studying multiple

---

[133] Professor Robert Cummings Neville, formerly the Dean of Theology at Boston University, presents an example of the practice of Confucian ideas and concepts in a non-Asian context in his book *Boston Confucianism* (2000).

wushu systems simultaneously can deepen our understanding of the effects of *gongfu* practice, through *wushu*, on various outcome variables. Multiple *wushu* systems can be examined simultaneously through the use of cross-case studies.

Cross-case studies

Multiple, or cross-case, studies (Miles and Huberman 1994; Miles, Huberman, and Saldaña 2014) can improve the generalizability of the findings of future research on Neo-Confucian learning through *wushu*. Multiple-case studies of *wushu* systems would provide confidence that the characteristics of Neo-Confucian learning under examination are generic in terms of their expected outcomes (Miles and Huberman 1994). Such studies could also examine the impact of Neo-Confucian learning practices for other arts—calligraphy, painting, poetry, music, and so forth—on effective daily living.[134] It is proposed here that the outcomes of various learning practices, including *wushu*, can be measured and assessed.

Outcome variables

There are several possible outcome variables that can be empirically examined in both single and multiple-case studies, as well as in traditional quantitative survey research (e.g., Kerlinger and Lee 2000). For instance, as mentioned earlier, adult ego development can be empirically measured utilizing the Washington University Sentence Completion Test, developed by Jane Loevinger (e.g., Hy and Loevinger 1996), for various Neo-Confucian practices.[135]

Several dimensions of positive psychology can be measured and evaluated in conjunction with Neo-Confucian learning practices, including, but not limited to, *wushu*. Positive psychology is a relatively recent

---

[134] Keep in mind that in traditional Chinese culture, virtually any practice can be considered an "art."

[135] Pfaffenberger, Marko, and Combs (2011) present excellent discussions of the assessment and description of higher, or postconventional, stages of ego development.

branch of psychology that focuses on making life more fulfilling. It is concerned with characteristics that enhance personal functioning, characteristics such as love, spirituality, optimism, and wisdom (Seligman and Csikszentmihalyi 2000; Seligman 2002).

Dimensions of positive psychology that can be considered and measured empirically—in conjunction with various *wushu* systems, as well as other Neo-Confucian learning practices—could include joy, contentment, love (Fredrickson 2002), well-being (Diener, Lucas, and Oishi 2002), compassion (Cassell 2002), forgiveness (McCullough and Witvliet 2002), empathy and altruism (Batson, Ahmad, Lishner, and Tsang 2002), humility (Tangney 2002), and wisdom (Baltes, Glück, and Kunzmann 2002). These are all attributes that Neo-Confucian learning is said to enhance over a long period of practice. Hypotheses can be developed to test these assertions in longitudinal studies over varying periods of time. Finally, outcome variables for practices from other traditions—such as yoga, Zen, and various devotional acts—can be measured, compared, and contrasted with Neo-Confucian practices for efficacy in different sample populations.

Final Thoughts

In a rapidly changing world of increasing complexity and interdependence, developing or expanding individual and collective consciousness is more crucial than ever before. As individuals expand their consciousness, or worldviews, they become capable of engaging in more effective problem-solving. As Tu Wei-ming suggests, "Learning to be human is to learn to be sensitive to an ever-expanding network of relationships" (1985, 175). This represents a process in which "the privatized ego is transformed into a feeling and caring self" (Tu 1983, 59). Less developed, or lower, levels of consciousness are often associated with youth and ego-centered behavior. In adult populations, individuals at this preconventional stage of development are focused on personal gain and advantage devoid of compassion. However, by expanding one's consciousness through self-effort over time, individual practitioners gradually move along the path of overcoming egotism, nepotism, parochialism, ethnocentrism, and chauvinistic nationalism, all of which represent varying degrees of human insensitivity (Tu 1985). Mencius felt that the structure of the heart-mind, if cultivated, is capable of unlimited expansion (Tu 1983). Therefore, knowing and preserving the heart-mind involves holding steadily to an ever-expanding structure (ibid.).

The present need for integrative, holistic thinking (Beck and Cohen 1996), as experienced in *guantong*, is apparent. In today's complex, interconnected environments, individuals, particularly leaders, must be comfortable with paradox, contradictions, and opposites (Kegan 1994). Contemporary leaders must be capable of comprehending multiple systems and perspectives simultaneously.

In a complex global environment, both leaders and individuals are being called upon to grasp not only the interdependence of systems, but they also must be able to understand patterns and interconnectedness across systems (Kegan 1994). In the areas of health, environment, and social systems, several critical topics call for such comprehensive understanding and thinking. For example, in the field of health care, leaders must recognize not only how challenges, such as cholera, Ebola virus, avian influenza, and drug-resistant strains of bacteria, could affect their own populations but they also must comprehend how such challenges can affect the global community. Leaders must be familiar with how climate change affects remote island nations, as well as how sea level change will affect large metropolitan areas. They must realize how poverty and lack of education impact underdeveloped nations and how mass migration impacts developed nations. They must recognize the connections among poverty, education, terrorism, and levels of consciousness. Ultimately, they must overcome the distinctions between self and other in their strategic analyses and planning.

This manuscript has attempted to describe one culture's traditional approach to ego development and the expansion of consciousness. The development and expansion of consciousness has been addressed by every culture to some degree. Facilitating the expansion of consciousness from egocentric, preconventional levels to conventional, socially desirable levels is the task of open-minded governments.[136] Now the task is to

---

[136] See Pfaffenberger, Marko, and Combs (2011) for an excellent discussion of postconventional stages of ego development.

encourage development to postconventional integral worldviews. This was one objective of the Cheng-Zhu School. Hence, this manuscript concludes with the following optimistic quote from Professor Tu Weiming of Peking University and Harvard.

> Our ability to transcend egoism, nepotism, parochialism, ethnocentrism, and chauvinistic nationalism must be extended to anthropocentrism as well. To make ourselves deserving partners of Heaven, we must constantly be in touch with that silent illumination that makes the rightness and principle in our heart-minds shine forth brilliantly. (1985, 180)

This is our collective aspiration.

GLOSSARY

Dao/Tao—the Way, path, way of proper conduct. This is the most basic term in Chinese philosophy, designating truth, ultimate reality, and the essence of all things.

Daoxue/tao-hsueh—learning of the Way as advocated in the Cheng-Zhu School of Neo-Confucian thought. This school became the orthodox philosophy and the basis for the civil-service examination system.

Gewu/ko-wu—investigation of things.

Gongfu/kungfu—methodical learning over time, which requires effort.

Guantong/kuan-t'ung—a state of consciousness in which individuals attain a comprehensive understanding, or integral consciousness, of situational contexts.

Jing/ching—inner mental attentiveness, reverence, seriousness, composure; a fully attentive mind.

Jingzuo/ching-tso—quiet sitting meditation.

Junzi/chü-tzu—the ideal or exemplary person.

Li—ritual propriety, etiquette, rules of proper behavior; rules that govern proper social relationships.

Li—coherence, principle, defining pattern; the valuable, intelligible way in which things fit together.

Liangzhi/liang-chih—innate knowledge of good, or innate moral intuition.

Qi/chi—vital energy.

Qiongli/ch'ing-li—exhaustive investigation of the principle in things and affairs.

Ren/jen—goodness, humanity, humaneness; the central virtue of Confucian philosophy.

Shen—spirit.

Shendu—being watchful over oneself when one is alone; vigilant solitariness.

Taiji/tai-chi—the Supreme Ultimate, the Supreme Polarity.

Tian/t'ien—Heaven, sky, blue sky.

Tianli/t'ien-li—Heavenly principle, ultimate principle.

Weifa/wei-fa—a state of pure consciousness before the rise of emotions.

Wushu—martial arts.

Xin/hsin—heart-mind; the psychological field of force that impacts the body; the mind generated from both positive and negative emotions.

Yifa/Yi-fa—a state of consciousness after the rise of emotions. This state can be harmonized.

Yin-yang—represented as opposites, such as positive and negative, light and dark, and male and female. These are relative, not absolute, concepts.

Zhi/chih—extension or increase.

Zhizhi/chih-chih—extending or the extension of knowledge.

REFERENCES

Adler, Joseph A. (2004). "Varieties of Spiritual Experience: Shen in Neo-Confucian Discourse." *Confucian Spirituality* 2: 120–148. Tu Weiming and Mary Evelyn Tucker, eds. New York: Crossroads.

Ames, Roger T. (1993). "On Body as Ritual Practice." *Self as Body in Asian Theory and Practice,* 149–156. T. P. Kasulis, R. T. Ames, and W. Dissanayake, eds. Albany, NY: State University of New York Press.

Ames, Roger T., and David L. Hall (2001). *Focusing the Familiar: A Translation and Philosophical Interpretation of the Zhongyong.* Honolulu: University of Hawaii Press.

Ames, Roger T., and David L. Hall (2003). *Daodejing, "Making This Life Significant": : A Philosophical Translation.* New York: Ballantine.

Ames, Roger T., and Henry Rosemont Jr. (1998). *The Analects of Confucius: A Philosophical Translation.* New York: Ballantine.

Angle, Stephen C. (2009). *Sagehood: The Contemporary Significance of Neo-Confucian Philosophy.* New York: Oxford University Press.

Austin, James H. (2000). "Consciousness Evolves When the Self Dissolves." *Cognitive Models and Spiritual Maps,* 209–230. J. Andresen and R. K. C. Forman, eds. Bowling Green, OH: Imprint Academic.

Baltes, Paul B., Judith Glück, and Ute Kunzmann (2002). "Wisdom: Its Structure and Function in Regulating Successful Life Span Development." *Handbook of Positive Psychology,* 327–347. C. R. Snyder and Shane J. Lopez, eds. New York: Oxford University Press.

Batson, C. Daniel, Nadia Ahmad, David A. Lishner, and Jo-Ann Tsang (2002). "Empathy and Altruism." *Handbook of Positive Psychology,* 485–498. C. R. Snyder and Shane J. Lopez, eds. New York: Oxford University Press.

Beck, Don. E., and Christopher Cowan (1996). *Spiral Dynamics: Mastering Values, Leadership and Change*. Malden, MA: Blackwell.

Berthong, John H. (2010). "Transmitting the Dao: Chinese Confucianism." *Confucianism in Context: Classic Philosophy and Contemporary Issues, East Asia and Beyond*, 9–31. Wonsuk Chang and Leah Kalmanson, eds. Albany, NY: State University of New York Press.

Berthong, John H., and Evelyn Nagai Berthong (2000). *Confucianism: A Short Introduction*. Boston: Oneworld.

Bloom, Irene (1985). "On the Matter of the Mind: The Metaphysical Basis of the Expanded Self." *Individualism and Holism: Studies in Confucian and Taoist Values*, 293–327. Donald Munro, ed. Ann Arbor, MI: Center for Chinese Studies, the University of Michigan.

Bloom, Irene (1999). "Mencius." *Sources of Chinese Tradition: From Earliest Times to 1600*, 114–158. Wm. Theodore de Bary and Irene Bloom, eds. New York: Columbia University Press.

Bol, Peter K. (1992). *"This Culture of Ours": Intellectual Transitions in T'ang and Sung China*. Stanford, CA: Stanford University Press.

Bol, Peter K. (2008). *Neo-Confucianism in History*. Cambridge, MA: Harvard University Asia Center, Harvard University Press.

Bruteau, Beatrice (1997). *God's Ecstasy: The Creation of a Self-Creating World*. New York: Crossroads.

Bruteau, Beatrice (2001). *The Grand Option: Personal Transformation and a New Creation*. Notre Dame, IN: University of Notre Dame Press.

Cassell, Eric J. (2002). "Compassion." *Handbook of Positive Psychology*, 434–445. C. R. Snyder and Shane J. Lopez, eds. New York: Oxford University Press.

Chan, Wing-Tsit (1963). *A Sourcebook in Chinese Philosophy*. Princeton, NJ: Princeton University Press.

Chan, Wing-Tsit (1987). *Chu Hsi: Life and Thought*. New York: St. Martin's.

Chen, Chun (1986). *Neo-Confucian Terms Explained by Ch'en Ch'un, 1159–1223*. Trans. Wing-tsit Chan. New York: Columbia University Press.

Cheng, Chung-ying (2003). "Qiongli (Ch'iung-li): Exhaustive Inquiry Into Principles." *Encyclopedia of Chinese Philosophy*, 623–625. Antonio S. Cua, ed. New York: Routledge.

Ching, Julia (1976). *To Acquire Wisdom: The Way of Wang Yang-ming.* New York: Columbia University Press.

Ching, Julia (1986a). "Chu Hsi on Personal Cultivation." *Chu Hsi and Neo-Confucianism,* 273–291. Wing-tsit Chan, ed. Honolulu: University of Hawaii Press.

Ching, Julia (1986b). "What Is Confucian Spirituality?" *Confucianism: The Dynamics of Tradition,* 63–80. Irene Eber, ed. New York: MacMillan.

Ching, Julia (2000). *The Religious Thought of Chu Hsi.* New York: Oxford University Press.

Ching, Julia (2003). "What Is Confucian Spirituality?" *Confucian Spirituality* 1: 81–95. Tu Weiming and Mary Evelyn Tucker, eds. New York: Crossroads.

Combs, Allan (1996). *The Radiance of Being: Complexity, Chaos and the Evolution of Consciousness.* St. Paul, MN: Paragon House.

Chow, David, and Richard Spangler (1982). *Kung Fu: History, Philosophy and Technique.* Burbank, CA: Unique Publications.

Csikszentmihalyi, Mihaly (1990). *Flow: The Psychology of Optimal Experience.* New York: HarperPerennial.

Csikszentmihalyi, Mihaly (1997). *Finding Flow: The Psychology of Engagement with Everyday Life.* New York: Basic Books.

Csikszentmihalyi, Mihaly (2003). *Good Business: Leadership, Flow, and the Making of Meaning.* New York: Viking Penguin.

Cua, Antonio S. (2003a). "Reason and Principle." *Encyclopedia of Chinese Philosophy,* 631–638. Antonio S. Cua, ed. New York: Routledge.

Cua, Antonio S. (2003b). "Wang Yangming (Wang Yang-ming)." *Encyclopedia of Chinese Philosophy,* 760–775. Antonia S. Cua, ed. New York: Routledge.

de Bary, Wm. Theodore (1970). "Introduction." *Self and Society in Ming Thought,* 1–28. Wm. Theodore de Bary, ed. New York: Columbia University Press.

de Bary, Wm. Theodore (1975). "Neo-Confucian Cultivation and the Seventeenth-Century 'Enlightenment'." *The Unfolding of Neo-Confucianism,* 141–216. New York: Columbia University Press.

de Bary, Wm. Theodore (1989). *The Message of the Mind in Neo-Confucianism.* New York: Columbia University Press.

de Bary, Wm. Theodore (1991). *Learning for One's Self.* New York: Columbia University Press.

de Bary, Wm. Theodore (2004). "Zhu Xi's Neo-Confucian Spirituality." *Confucian Spirituality* 2: 72–98. Tu Weiming and Mary Evelyn Tucker, eds. New York: Crossroads.

de Bary, Wm. Theodore and Irene Bloom, eds. (1999). *Sources of Chinese Tradition: From Earliest Times to 1600* Vol. 1, 2nd ed. New York: Columbia University Press.

Diener, Ed, Richard E. Lucas, and Shigehiro Oishi (2002). "Subjective Well-Being: The Science of Happiness and Life Satisfaction." *Handbook of Positive Psychology,* 63–73. C. R. Snyder and Shane J. Lopez, eds. New York: Oxford University Press.

East Asian History Sourcebook: Wang Yang-ming: From the Philosophy, c. 1525. http://www.fordham.edu/halsall/eastasia/wangyang1.html, (3/2/2009). Bronx, NY: Fordham University.

Elvin, Mark (1993). "Tales of Shen and Xin: Body-Person and Heart-Mind in China During the Last 150 Years." *Self as Body in Asian Theory and Practice,* 213–291. T. P. Kasulis, ed. Albany, NY: State University of New York Press.

Feuerstein, Georg (1997). *Lucid Waking: Mindfulness and the Spiritual Potential of Humanity.* Rochester, VT: Inner Traditions International.

Fredrickson, Barbara J. (2002). "Positive Emotions." *Handbook of Positive Psychology,* 120–134. C. R. Snyder and Shane J. Lopez, eds. New York: Oxford University Press.

Ferrer, Jorge N. (2000). "The Perennial Philosophy Revisited." *Journal of Transpersonal Psychology* 32: 7–30.

Fingarette, Herbert (1972). *Confucius: The Secular as Sacred.* Reissued 1988. Prospect Heights, IL: Waveland Press.

Fischer-Schreiber, Ingrid, Franz-Karl Ehrhard, Kurt Friedrichs, and Michael S. Diener (1994). *The Encyclopedia of Eastern Philosophy and Religion.* Boston: Shambhala.

Frisina, Warren G. (2002). *The Unity of Knowledge and Actions: Towards a Nonrepresentational Theory of Knowledge.* Albany, NY: SUNY Press.

Fung, Yu-lan (1983). *A History of Chinese Philosophy, Vol. 2: The Period of Classical Learning.* Princeton: Princeton University Press.

Gardner, Daniel K. (1986). *Chu Hsi and the Ta-hsueh: Neo-Confucian Reflection on the Confucian Canon.* Cambridge, MA: Harvard University Press.

Gardner, Daniel K. (1990). *Chu Hsi Learning to Be a Sage: Selections from the Conversations of Master Chu, Arranged Topically.* Berkeley, CA: University of California Press.

Gardner, Daniel K. (2004). "Attentiveness and Meditative Reading in Cheng-Zhu Neo-Confucianism." *Confucian Spirituality* 2: 99–110. Tu Weiming and Mary Evelyn Tucker, eds. New York: Crossroads.

Gebser, Jean (1985). *The Ever-Present Origin.* Trans. Noel Barstad with Algis Mickunas. Athens, OH: Ohio University Press.

Gotshalk, Richard (1999). *The Beginnings of Philosophy in China.* Lanham, MD: University Press of America.

Graham, Angus Charles (A. C.) (1985). *Reason and Spontaneity: A New Solution to the Problem of Fact and Value,* 52–60. London: Curzon Press.

Graham, A. C. (1992). *Two Chinese Philosophers: The Metaphysics of the Brothers Ch'eng.* La Salle, IL: Open Court.

Great Learning, http://en.wikipedia.org/wiki/Great_Learning (3/2/2009).

Gwin, Peter (2011). "Kung Fu Kingdom: Battle for the Soul of Kung Fu," *National Geographic* 219, no. 3: 94–113.

Hall, David L., and Roger T. Ames (1987). *Thinking Through Confucius.* Albany, NY: State University of New York Press.

Hall, David L., and Roger T. Ames (1998). "Chinese Philosophy." *Routledge Encyclopedia of Philosophy.* E. Craig, ed. London: Routledge. http://www.rep.routledge.com/article/G001SECT9 (3/3/2009).

Heidegger, Martin (1966). *Discourse on Thinking.* New York: Harper.

Hennessy, Mark (1995). *Cheng Man-ch'ing: Master of Five Excellences.* Berkley, CA: Frog.

Hinton, David (1998a). *The Analects: Confucius.* Washington, DC: Counterpoint.

Hinton, David. (1998b) *Mencius.* Washington, DC: Counterpoint.

Huxley, Aldous (1945). *The Perennial Philosophy.* New York: Harper and Row.

Hsu, Adam (1997). *The Sword Polisher's Record: The Way of Kung-Fu.* Rutland, VT: Tuttle.

Huang, Siu-chi (1999). *Essentials of Neo-Confucianism: Eight Major Philosophers of the Song and Ming Periods.* Westport, CT: Greenwood Press.

Hy, Lê Xuân, and Jane Loevinger (1996). *Measuring Ego Development,* 2nd ed. Mahwah, NJ: Lawrence Erlbaum.

James, William (1941). *The Varieties of Religious Experience: A Study in Human Nature.* New York: Longmans, Green and Co.

Jing zuo, http://en.wikipedia.org/wiki/Jing_zuo (3/2/2009).

Kalton, Michael C. (2004). "Sage Learning." *Confucian Spirituality* 2: 183–203. Tu Weiming and Mary Evelyn Tucker, eds. New York: Crossroads.

Kaptchuk, Ted J. (2000). *The Web That Has No Weaver: Understanding Chinese Medicine.* New York: McGraw-Hill.

Keenan, Barry C. (2011). *Neo-Confucian Self-Cultivation.* Honolulu: University of Hawai'i Press.

Kegan, Robert (1994). *In Over Our Heads: The Mental Demands of Modern Life.* Cambridge, MA: Harvard University Press.

Kerlinger, Fred N., and Howard B. Lee (2000). *Foundations of Behavioral Research* 4th ed. South Melbourne, Australia: Wadsworth Thomson Learning.

Kim, Hansang A. (2013). "Freedom, Agency and the Primacy of Li in Zhu Xi's Neo-Confucianism (Seongnihak)." *The Review of Korean Studies* 16, no. 1: 121–135.

Kim, Yung Sik (2000). *The Natural Philosophy of Chu Hsi (1130–1200).* Philadelphia: American Philosophical Society.

Kuo, Simmone (1996). *Shao-Lin Chuan: The Rhythm and Power of Tan-Tui.* Berkeley, CA: North Atlantic Books.

Kohlberg, Lawrence (1986). "A Current Statement on Some Theoretical Issues." *Lawrence Kolhberg: Consensus and Controversy,* 485–546. Sohan Modgil and Celia Modgil, eds. London: Falmer Press.

Kohlberg, Lawrence and R. A. Ryncarz (1990). "Beyond Justice Reasoning: Moral Development and Consideration of a Seventh Stage." In *Higher Stages of Adult Human Development: Perspectives on Adult Growth,* 191–207. Charles N. Alexander and Ellen Langer, eds. New York: Oxford University Press.

Lee, Bruce (1997). *The Tao of Gung Fu: A Study in the Way of Chinese Martial Art.* John Little, ed. Boston: Charles E. Tuttle.

Lee, Bruce, and M. Uyehara (2008). *Bruce Lee's Fighting Methods: The Complete Edition.* Sarah Dzida, Jon Sattler, and Jeannie Santiago, eds. Burbank, CA: Black Belt Books, Ohara Publications.

Lee, Jig-chuen (1987). "Wang Yang-ming, Chu Hsi, and the Investigation of Things." *Philosophy East and West* 37, no. 1: 24–35.

Li, Tu (2003). "Tang Junyi (T'ang Chün-i)." *Encyclopedia of Chinese Philosophy,* 712–716. Antonio S. Cua, ed. New York: Routledge.

Liang, Weiming, and Jieping He (2010). *Iconographic Dictionary of Chinese Traditional Kung-Fu.* Hong Kong: Tin Wu Press.

Liang, Shou-Yu, and Wen-Ching Wu (1977). *Qigong Empowerment: A Guide to Medical, Taoist, Buddhist, and Wushu Energy Cultivation.* East Providence, RI: The Way of the Dragon.

Lin, Tongqi (2004). "Mou Zongsan's Spiritual Vision: How Is 'Summum Bonum' Possible?" *Confucian Spirituality* 2: 323–352. Tu Weiming and Mary Ellen Tucker, eds. New York: Crossroads.

Liu, Shu-hsien (2003). *Essentials of Contemporary Neo-Confucian Philosophy.* Westport, CT: Praeger.

Liu, Shu-hsien (2004). "Contemporary Neo-Confucian Philosophy." *Confucian Spirituality* 2: 353–376. Tu Weiming and Mary Ellen Tucker, eds. New York: Crossroads.

Liu, Tianjun, ed. (2010). *Chinese Medical Qigong.* Philadelphia: Singing Dragon.

Logsdon, Jeanne M., and John E. Young (2005). "Executive Influence on Ethical Culture: Self-transcendence, Differentiation, and Integration." *Positive Psychology in Business Ethics and Corporate Responsibility,* 103–122. Robert A. Giacalone, Carole L. Jurkiewicz, and Craig Dunn, eds. Greenwich, CN: Information Age.

Makeham, John, ed. (2003). "The Retrospective Creation of New Confucianism." *New Confucianism: A Critical Examination,* 25–55. New York: Palgrave MacMillan.

Marcel, Gabriel (1948). *The Philosophy of Existence.* Trans. Manya Haraim. London: Harvill Press.

McCullough, Michael E., and Charlotte V. Witvliet (2002). "The Psychology of Forgiveness." *Handbook of Positive Psychology,*

446–458. C. R. Snyder and Shane J. Lopez, eds. New York: Oxford University Press.

Miles, Matthew B., and A. Michael Huberman (1994). *Qualitative Data Analysis: An Expanded Sourcebook*, 2nd ed. Thousand Oaks, CA: Sage Publications.

Miles, Matthew B., A. Michael Huberman, and Johnny Saldaña (2014). *Qualitative Data Analysis: A Methods Sourcebook*, 3rd ed. Thousand Oaks, CA: Sage Publications.

Munro, Donald (2005). *A Chinese Ethics for the New Century: The Ch'ien Mu Lectures in History and Culture, and Other Essays on Science and Confucian Ethics*. Hong Kong: The Chinese University Press.

Munro, Donald (2008). "Challenges and Arguments, Interview by Liu Xiaogan." *Ethics in Action: Workable Guidelines for Private and Public Choices*, 93–133. Hong Kong: The Chinese University Press.

Neo-Confucian Learning and Wang Yangming (1472–1529), http://www.iun.edu/~hisdcl/h425/wangyangming.htm (11/11/2014).

Neville, Robert C. (2000). *Boston Confucianism: Portable Tradition in the Late-Modern World*. Albany, NY: State University of New York Press.

Ng, William Yau-nang (2004). "Tang Junyi's Spirituality: Reflections on Its Foundation and Possible Contemporary Relevance." *Confucian Spirituality* 2: 377–398. Tu Weiming and Mary Evelyn Tucker, eds. New York: Crossroads.

Ni, Peimin (1996). "A Qigong Interpretation of Confucianism." *Journal of Chinese Philosophy* 23, no. 1: 79–97.

Ni, Peimin (2008). "Gongfu—A Vital Dimension of Confucian Teaching." *Confucius Now: Contemporary Encounters with the Analects*, 167–187. David Jones, ed. Chicago and La Salle, IL: Open Court.

Norman, D. A. (1983). "Some Observations on Mental Models." *Mental Models*, 7–14. D. Genter and A. L. Stevens, eds. Hillsdale, NJ: Erlbaum.

Pfaffenberger, Angela H., Paul W. Marko, and Alan Combs, eds. (2011). *The Postconventional Personality: Assessing, Researching, and Theorizing Higher Development*. Albany, NY: State University of New York Press.

Podgorski, Frank (1985). "Two Models of Spiritual Journey: Yoga and Confucius." *Journal of Chinese Philosophy* 12: 23–47.

Puhakka, Kaisa (1998). "Contemplating Everything: Wilber's Evolutionary Theory in Dialectical Perspective." *Ken Wilber in Dialogue: Conversations With Leading Transpersonal Thinkers*, 283–304. D. Rothberg and S. Kelly, eds. Wheaton, IL: Theosophical Publishing House.

Reid, Daniel (2000). *A Complete Guide to Chi-Gung*. Boston: Shambhala.

Reid, Howard, and Michael Croucher (1995). *The Way of the Warrior: The Paradox of the Martial Arts*. London: Leopard Books.

Rošker, Jana S. (2012). *Traditional Chinese Philosophy and the Paradigm of Structure (Li)*. Newcastle Upon Tyne, UK: Cambridge Scholars Publishing.

Seligman, Martin E. P., and Mihaly Csikszentmihalyi (2000). "Positive Psychology: An Introduction." *American Psychologist* 55: 5–14.

Seligman, Martin E. P. (2002). "Positive Psychology, Positive Prevention, and Positive Therapy." *Handbook of Positive Psychology*, 3–9. C. R. Snyder and Shane J. Lopez, eds. New York: Oxford University Press.

Shen, Vincent (2003). "Ren (Jen): Humanity." *Encyclopedia of Chinese Philosophy:* 643–646. Antonio S. Cua, ed. New York: Routledge.

Tangney, June Price (2002). "Humility." *Handbook of Positive Psychology*, 411–419. C. R. Snyder and Shane J. Lopez, eds. New York: Oxford University Press.

Taylor, Rodney L. (2005). *The Illustrated Encyclopedia of Confucianism*. New York: Rosen.

Tu, Wei-ming (1983). "The Idea of the Human in Mencian Thought: An Approach to Chinese Aesthetics." *Theories of the Arts in China*, 57–73. Susan Bush and Christian Murck, eds. Princeton, NJ: Princeton University Press.

Tu, Wei-ming (1985). *Confucian Thought: Selfhood as Creative Transformation*. Albany, NY: State University of New York Press.

Tu, Wei-ming (1986). "Toward a Third Epoch of Confucianism." *Confucianism: The Dynamics of Tradition*, 3–21. Irene Eber, ed. New York: MacMillan.

Tu, Wei-ming (1989). *Centrality and Commonality: An Essay on Confucian Religiousness*. Albany, NY: State University of New York Press.

Tu, Wei-ming (1993). *Way, Learning, and Politics: Essays on the Confucian Intellectual*. Albany, NY: State University of New York.

Tu, Wei-ming (1998). *Humanity and Self-Cultivation: Essays in Confucian Thought.* Boston: Cheng & Tsui.

Tu, Weiming (2004). "Learning to Be Human: Spiritual Exercises from Zhu Xi and Wang Yangming to Liu Zangzhou." *Confucian Spirituality* 2: 149–162. Tu Weiming and Mary Evelyn Tucker, eds. New York: Crossroads.

Tu, Weiming and Mary Ellen Tucker, eds. (2004). *Confucian Spirituality* 2, New York: Crossroads.

Watson, Burton (2007). *The Analects of Confucius.* New York: Columbia University Press.

Wilber, Ken (1985). *The Holographic Paradigm and Other Paradoxes.* Ken Wilber, ed. Boston: Shambhala.

Wilber, Ken (1993). "Psychologia Perennis: The Spectrum of Consciousness." *Paths Beyond Ego: The Transpersonal Vision,* 21–33. Roger Walsh and Frances Vaughan, eds. New York: Penguin Putnam.

Wilber, Ken (1999). "Integral Psychology." *The Collected Works of Ken Wilber* 4: 423–717, Boston: Shambhala.

Wilber, Ken (2000). "Waves, Streams, States and Self: Further Consideration for an Integral Theory of Consciousness." *Cognitive Models and Spiritual Maps,* 145–176. Jensine Andresen and Robert K. C. Forman, eds. Bowling Green, OH: Imprint Academic.

Wu-Monnat, Grace (1998). "Growing Up With Wang Ziping & Madam Wang Jurong." *Qigong Kungfu,* July: 27–54.

Yao, Xinzhong (2000). *An Introduction to Confucianism.* Cambridge, UK: Cambridge University Press.

Yang, Jwing-ming (2003). *Taijiquan Theory of Dr. Yang Jwing-ming: The Root of Taijiquan.* Boston: YMAA.

Yang, Jwing-ming, and Jeffery A. Bolt (1982). *Shaolin Long Fist Kung Fu.* Burbank, CA: Unique Publications.

Young, John E. (2002). "A Spectrum of Consciousness for CEOs: A Business Application of Ken Wilber's Spectrum of Consciousness." *The International Journal of Organizational Analysis* 10 (1): 30–54.

Young, John E., and Janice B. Corzine (2004). "The Sage Entrepreneur: A Review of Traditional Confucian Practices Applied to Contemporary Entrepreneurship." *Journal of Enterprising Culture* 12 (1): 79–104.

Young, John E., and Jeanne M. Logsdon (2005). "Integral Sensemaking for Executives: The Evolution of Spiritually-based Integral Consciousness." *Journal of Management, Spirituality & Religion* 2 (1): 67–103. Reprinted in *At Work: Spirituality Matters* (2007): 191–226. J. Biberman and M. D. Whitty, eds. Scranton, PA: The University of Scranton Press.

Zhang, Dainian (2002). *Key Concepts in Chinese Philosophy*. Trans. Edmund Ryden. New Haven, CT: Yale University Press.

Zhu, Xi (1997). *Classified Conversations of Master Zhu*. Changsha: Yuelu Shushe. (Cited in Stephen C. Angle 2009).

NOTES

NOTES

NOTES

NOTES

ABOUT THE AUTHOR

John E. Young, Ph.D., is professor emeritus at the Anderson School of Management at the University of New Mexico, where he taught entrepreneurship, and also strategic management based on Sun Tzu's *Art of War*. His research includes the topics of entrepreneurial learning, Confucian learning, and levels of consciousness. He practices *taijiquan* (barehand and weapons), *Shaolin* (barehand and weapons), *chaquan,* and *tan tui.* He also studies the Filipino martial arts of *escrema* and *kuntao (kuntau).* John teaches *taijiquan* as well as external *kungfu*, primarily to seniors, in Albuquerque, New Mexico, USA.

Printed in the United States
By Bookmasters